my **revision** notes

OCR A-level History

RUSSIA AND ITS RULERS

1855–1964

Andrew Holland

Series Editor
Nick Fellows

 **HODDER** EDUCATION
AN HACHETTE UK COMPANY

Acknowledgements

The Publishers would like to thank the following for permission to reproduce copyright material. **pp.79 & 94** *Russia 1855–1991: From Tsars to Commissars* by Peter Oxley (OUP, 2001), copyright © Peter Oxley 2001, reprinted by permission of Oxford University Press.; **pp.84 & 94** *Endurance and Endeavour: Russian History 1812–2000* by J. N. Westwood (2000): 311 words (p. 66 and p. 224). By permission of Oxford University Press.; **p.91** Siobhan Peeling, 'Provisional Government', 1914–1918-online. International Encyclopedia of the First World War.

Every effort has been made to trace all copyright holders, but if any have been inadvertently overlooked, the Publishers will be pleased to make the necessary arrangements at the first opportunity.

Although every effort has been made to ensure that website addresses are correct at the time of going to press, Hodder Education cannot be held responsible for the content of any website mentioned in this book. It is sometimes possible to find a relocated web page by typing in the address of the home page for a website in the URL window of your browser.

Hachette UK's policy is to use papers that are natural, renewable and recyclable products and made from wood grown in well-managed forests and other controlled sources. The logging and manufacturing processes are expected to conform to the environmental regulations of the country of origin.

Orders: please contact Hachette UK Distribution, Hely Hutchinson Centre, Milton Road, Didcot, Oxfordshire, OX11 7HH. Telephone: +44 (0)1235 827827. Email education@hachette.co.uk Lines are open from 9 a.m. to 5 p.m., Monday to Friday. You can also order through our website: www.hoddereducation.co.uk

ISBN: 978 1 4718 7591 5

© Andrew Holland 2017

First published in 2017 by

Hodder Education,

An Hachette UK Company

Carmelite House

50 Victoria Embankment

London EC4Y 0DZ

www.hoddereducation.co.uk

Impression number   10 9 8 7

Year   2022

Cover photo © Lawrence Manning/Corbis
Illustrations by Integra
Typeset by Integra Software Services Pvt. Ltd., Pondicherry, India
Printed in India

A catalogue record for this title is available from the British Library.

My Revision Planner

REVISED

REVISED

4

Introduction

Unit 3: Thematic study and historical interpretation

Unit 3 in the OCR A-level specification involves the thematic study of topics over a period of at least 100 years, and three Depth Studies of events, individuals or issues that are key parts of the overall theme. You will be expected to view the theme synoptically. In other words you should be able to summarise developments by synthesising or making links between events over the whole period. You will also need to be able to discern patterns of change and continuity and similarity and difference over the whole period before arriving at judgements based on your observations. In the in-depth section you will be expected to apply your contextual knowledge to evaluate two interpretations and reach a supported judgement as to which one you consider to be the most valid.

Russia and its Rulers, 1855–1964: content

The following is a list of the main Key Topics you will study within the theme.
- Key Topic 1 – The nature of government
- Key Topic 2 – The impact of dictatorial regimes on the economy and society of the Russian Empire and the USSR
- Key Topic 3 – The impact of war and revolution on the development of the Russian Empire and the USSR
- Key Topic 4 – Russia: Empire, nationalities and satellite states.

The Depth Studies topics are:
- Alexander II's domestic reforms
- The Provisional Government
- Khrushchev in power, 1956–64.

Examination requirements

The examination paper will be divided into two sections, Section A and Section B. Section A will contain a question on interpretations and Section B will provide essay questions. The examination lasts two and a half hours, and you are advised to spend an hour on Section A and one and a half hours on Section B, which will give you 45 minutes for each essay.

The A-level examination at the end of the course can cover any of the Key Topic and Depth Study content. You are required to answer ONE Depth Study question, for which there is NO choice, and TWO Key Topic essays from a choice of THREE. Unit 3 is worth a total of 80 marks and 40 per cent of the final A-level marks.

In the A-level examination you are being tested on your ability to:
- use relevant historical information to support arguments
- handle historical concepts, especially change/continuity and similarity/difference
- write synoptically using synthesis
- analyse and evaluate a range of factors before reaching a balanced judgement
- analyse and evaluate interpretations made by historians.

How to use this book

There are two strands to the book, which have been designed to help you develop the knowledge and skills necessary to succeed in the examination.
- The main part of the book is divided into seven sections – each of the first four sections covers a Key Topic and the last three sections deal with the three Depth Studies.
- The Key Topic and Depth Study sections are organised into double-page spreads.
- On the left-hand page you will find a summary of the key content you will need to learn.
- On the right-hand page you will find exam-focused activities.

Note that words in bold in the key content are defined in the glossary (see page 106)

▼ **Key historical content**

▼ **Exam-focused activities**

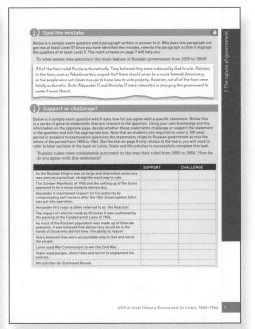

Examination activities

There are three levels of exam-focused activities:

- Band 1 activities are designed to develop the foundation skills needed to pass the exam. These have a green heading and this symbol:
- Band 2 activities are designed to build on the skills developed in Band 1 activities and to help you to achieve a C grade. These have an orange heading and this symbol:
- Band 3 activities are designed to enable you to access the highest grades. These have a purple heading and this symbol:

Some of the activities have answers or suggested answers that can be found online at www.hoddereducation.co.uk/myrevisionnotes. These have the following symbol to indicate this:

Each section ends with exam-style questions and sample answers with commentary. This will give you guidance on what is expected to achieve the top grade.

You can also keep track of your revision by ticking off each topic heading in the book, or by ticking the checklist on the contents page. Tick each box when you have:

- revised and understood a topic
- completed the activities.

Mark schemes

For some of the activities in the book it will be useful to refer to the mark scheme for this paper. Below is an abbreviated form.

A-level

Level	Historical Interpretation	Thematic Essay
6	Well-focused answer, aware of the wider debate with detailed knowledge used to evaluate the interpretations and reach a judgement. [26–30]	Very good focus and clear argument with developed synthesis across the period to reach a substantiated judgement. [21–25]
5	Good focus, with some awareness of the wider debate and uses good knowledge to evaluate the interpretations and reach a judgement. [21–25]	Good focus and argument with some synthesis across the period to reach a developed judgement. [17–20]
4	Mostly focused with awareness of the wider debate and uses some knowledge to evaluate the interpretations and produce a judgement. [16–20]	Mostly focused argument with limited synthesis across the period to reach a limited judgement. [13–16]
3	Partially focused with limited awareness of the wider debate and limited knowledge used to evaluate the interpretations. [11–15]	Partial focus and argument with undeveloped synthesis across the period to reach a judgement which is poorly supported. [9–12]
2	Limited focus and awareness of the wider debate and uses limited knowledge to evaluate but relies on information from the passages. [6–10]	Limited focus and argument with a judgement which is not well linked to the explanation. [5–8]
1	The answer is focused more on the topic than the question and there is description of the interpretations. [1–5]	Limited focus on the topic and is mostly descriptive with a judgement that is asserted. [1–4]

1 The nature of government

Autocracy

Russia was governed by an **autocracy** from 1855 to March 1917. Some historians have argued that there were three aspects to Russian autocracy:

- Tsars believed they were accountable only to God and not to the people. Hence, there was no need for democratic elections.
- Tsars also believed that God had placed them on Earth to set moral standards. They had a paternalistic duty to ensure that 'the people' were protected from the more evil elements in society.
- As the Russian Empire was so large and diversified, autocracy was seen as a practical, straightforward way to rule. Advisers to the government such as **Konstantin Pobedonostsev** argued that **liberal democracy** would have led to too many people demanding too many things. Also, as most of the Russian population was made up of illiterate peasants, it was believed that democracy would be in the hands of those who did not have 'the ability to reason'.

Autocracy, repression and reform

The tsars used their autocratic power differently according to circumstance. However, they all reinforced autocracy through a mixture of **repression** and **reform**.

- **Nicholas I (Tsar 1825–55)** had promoted autocratic rule through the use of slogans such as 'Orthodoxy, Autocracy and Nationality'. 'Orthodoxy' indicated an intention not to make radical changes, 'autocracy' suggested that there would be complete obedience to the Tsar and 'nationality' emphasised the need to create a united Russia based on the traditions and values of the original **Rus peoples**. It was reinforced with the passing of the **Fundamental Laws of 1832** which stated that 'The emperor of all the Russians is an autocratic and unlimited monarch'.
- **Alexander II (Tsar 1855–81)** stuck closely to autocratic principles, especially after the first attempt to assassinate him in 1866. Although Alexander II was a willing reformer, his policies were still carried out with the need to preserve autocracy in mind. For example, he maintained respect for his authority by compensating **serf** owners after the 1861 Emancipation Edict (see page 20) was put into operation.
- **Alexander III (Tsar 1881–94)** reigned with what is often viewed as more intense authoritarian rule. It is often referred to as 'the Reaction' – a response against the more reforming period of his father's rule. Alexander strongly believed that the **Slav peoples** lacked the intelligence to participate responsibly in a democratic political system. Besides, they were viewed as displaying 'inertness and laziness' and were therefore undeserving of greater freedoms. Nevertheless, like his father, he was willing to reform if it benefited Russia as a whole.
- **Nicholas II (Tsar 1894–1917)** continued the rather severe form of autocratic rule adopted by his father. The **October Manifesto** of 1905 and the setting up of the *Duma* (see page 14) appeared to be a move towards democracy. The impact of these reforms, though, was cushioned by the passing of the autocratic **Fundamental Laws of 1906**.

! Spot the mistake

Below is a sample exam question and a paragraph written in answer to it. Why does this paragraph not get into at least Level 5? Once you have identified the mistake, rewrite the paragraph so that it displays the qualities of at least Level 5. The mark scheme on page 7 will help you.

> To what extent was autocracy the main feature of Russian government from 1855 to 1964?

> All of the tsars ruled Russia autocratically. They believed they were ordained by God to rule. Advisers to the tsars, such as Pobedonostsev, argued that there should never be a move towards democracy as the people were not clever enough to know how to vote properly. However, not all of the tsars were totally autocratic. Both Alexander II and Nicholas II were interested in changing the government to make it more liberal.

! Support or challenge?

Below is a sample exam question which asks how far you agree with a specific statement. Below this is a series of general statements that are relevant to the question. Using your own knowledge and the information on the opposite page, decide whether these statements challenge or support the statement in the question and tick the appropriate box. Note that as students are required to cover a 100-year period in answers to examination questions the statements relate to Russian government across the whole of the period from 1855 to 1964. But the text on page 8 only relates to the tsars; you will need to refer to later sections in the book on Lenin, Stalin and Khrushchev to successfully complete this task.

> 'Russian rulers were consistently autocratic in the way they ruled from 1855 to 1964.' How far do you agree with this statement?

	SUPPORT	CHALLENGE
As the Russian Empire was so large and diversified, autocracy was seen as a practical, straightforward way to rule.		
The October Manifesto of 1905 and the setting up of the *Duma* appeared to be a move towards democracy.		
Alexander II maintained respect for his authority by compensating serf owners after the 1861 Emancipation Edict was put into operation.		
Alexander III's reign is often referred to as 'the Reaction'.		
The impact of reforms made by Nicholas II was cushioned by the passing of the Fundamental Laws of 1906.		
As most of the Russian population was made up of illiterate peasants, it was believed that democracy would be in the hands of those who did not have 'the ability to reason'.		
Tsars believed they were accountable only to God and not to the people.		
Lenin used War Communism to win the Civil War.		
Stalin used purges, show trials and terror to implement his policies.		
Khrushchev de-Stalinised Russia.		

Dictatorship

Russia was governed by a form of **dictatorship** after the **October Revolution** of 1917. The leader of the dictatorship, **Lenin**, based his ideology of government on the work of **Karl Marx** (1818–83) and **Friedrich Engels** (1820–95). The ideology, **Marxism–Leninism**, centred on two key principles:

- The '**superstructure**' of institutions that formed the base for the old tsarist society had to be destroyed and replaced with bodies that would create an **egalitarian society**.
- Marx's 'Labour Theory of Value' became a justification for Lenin to overthrow tsarist rule, especially as the tsars had started to move towards **capitalism**.

The 'Labour Theory of Value'

This theory claimed that under a capitalist economy the **proletariat** would never gain the full value of their efforts. A disproportionate amount of wages would be taken away to provide capitalists with profits far in excess of what was needed to maintain industrialisation. In other words, the proletariat would be exploited by capitalists.

Marx outlined how a struggle between the capitalists and workers would result from exploitation – the prediction was that a government consisting only of workers would be formed. More specifically:

- Workers would eventually be successful in overthrowing the capitalists.
- In the short term, intellectuals such as Lenin would be needed to help the workers govern.
- Once the proletariat became more politically educated then a **dictatorship of the proletariat** would occur (that is, rule over the **bourgeoisie** by the workers).

Implementation of Marxism–Leninism

Lenin implemented his ideology by:

- passing on his views through his writings. Most important was the publication of *What is to be Done?* (1902), in which Lenin argued the need for revolutionaries to bypass the implementation of a democratically elected assembly and go straight to a government led by a **Party Central Committee**. Lenin believed this was necessary as in a system where workers might be given the vote they would not have the political knowledge and experience to use it in a way that would result in revolutionary change to their position in society. Therefore a Bolshevik cadre (or Committee), versed in Marxism, needed to be appointed to make decisions on behalf of workers. The Committee would govern until the workers were ready to take over.
- leading a Bolshevik revolution against the **Provisional Government** in October 1917.
- engaging in a civil war, from 1917 to 1921, against the opponents of the revolution (the **Whites**).
- using **War Communism** to ensure that there was no drift from his close followers or those he perceived should have supported Marxism–Leninism – proletarians and peasants. War Communism was implemented with a degree of ruthlessness similar to that used by Alexander III when he attempted **Russification** (see page 64). Both Alexander III and Lenin used the secret police (the **Okhrana** and the **Cheka** respectively) to enforce their policies brutally.
- making concessions in the form of the **New Economic Policy (NEP)** after the Civil War seemed to be won. This was done to ensure the backing of moderate **Bolsheviks** but it caused something of a split in the party. **Trotsky** believed the Bolsheviks should have quickly moved away from appeasing bourgeois elements through the NEP. He wanted a more '**permanent revolution**', which meant the spreading of communism throughout the world. Others, such as **Bukharin**, disagreed and believed that the NEP was probably a necessary temporary measure to enable the consolidation of '**socialism in one country**'.

! Delete as applicable   a

Below is a sample exam question and a paragraph of an answer to it. Read the paragraph and decide which of the possible options (in bold) is most appropriate. Delete the least appropriate options and complete the paragraph by justifying your selection.

> To what extent did the communist dictators govern in the same way as the tsars from 1855 to 1964?

Lenin's rule was similar to that of all the tsars to a **limited/fair/great** extent in that he was solely in charge. He also used repressive measures, like the tsars, such as War Communism. War Communism was implemented with a **reasonable/considerable** degree of ruthlessness very similar to that used by Alexander III when he attempted Russification. Also, Lenin was similar to **all/some** of the tsars in the way in which he used reforms to appease the people. Thus Alexander II emancipated the serfs to give them greater economic freedoms and Lenin introduced the NEP, which provided opportunities for peasants to trade freely and set up their own businesses. Thus, Lenin, in comparison to the tsars, **partly continued/continued** the way Russia was ruled as he. . .

_____

_____

⚡ Identify an argument   a

Below are a series of definitions, a sample exam question and two sample conclusions. One of the conclusions achieves a high-level mark because it contains an argument. The other achieves a lower level because it contains only description and assertion. Identify which is which. The mark scheme on page 7 will help you.

- **Description**: a detailed account
- **Assertion**: a statement of fact or an opinion, which is not supported by a reason
- **Reason**: a statement that explains or justifies something
- **Argument**: an assertion justified with a reason

> 'Lenin's seizure of power in 1917 was the most important turning point in the development of Russian government from 1855 to 1964.' How far do you agree with this statement?

Lenin's seizure of power in October 1917 was undoubtedly a major turning point as it marked the end of an attempt to introduce the Constituent Assembly. It also represented the beginning of a move, in theory, towards rule by the proletariat ('the dictatorship of the proletariat') and a more egalitarian society in general. However, without the problems caused by the First World War and subsequent February Revolution of 1917 there would have been no Provisional Government and no attempt to install a Constituent Assembly in the first place. Lenin was able to exploit the problems of the Provisional Government to gain power. Therefore it was Russia's involvement in the First World War that was the most important turning point in Russian government from 1855 to 1964.

After Lenin seized power in October 1917 he went on to introduce communism to Russia and created a dictatorship. This was very different from the tsars. He consolidated his power by winning the Civil War of 1917–21 and through the introduction of War Communism. He was also important for developing his New Economic Policy, which improved the lives of Russians. Some historians disagree, though, that Lenin's seizure of power was the most important turning point because he carried on using repressive policies like the tsars. In other words, he was just a 'Red Tsar'.

Totalitarianism

After Lenin's death in 1924 a power struggle ensued. **Stalin** skilfully manipulated various individuals and factions to gain support for his takeover of the leadership of the Soviet Union. From 1928 onwards Stalin redefined Marxism–Leninism and moved Russia towards a totalitarian state. There were two main strands to Stalin's ideology:

- The implementation of a **command economy**, based on centralised planning and **collectivisation** so that the superstructure of society could be changed.
- The personalisation of the superstructure so that total control of the economy, society and politics was in the hands of one person – Stalin. This was to be achieved through the artful use of propaganda (including the development of the **cult of personality**), increased censorship and repression of opposition on a scale never witnessed before.

Stalin and totalitarianism

There are a number of possible explanations as to why Stalin moved Russia away from a Lenin-style dictatorship to **totalitarianism**.

- He exploited circumstances to implement a practical solution to Russia's problems. For his **Five-Year Plans** and collectivisation to be successful, no one could be allowed to question whether the policies were appropriate.
- Another view is that Stalin was a megalomaniac. He did whatever was needed to gain and maintain power to fuel his desire to appear important.
- A more recent idea is that Stalin intentionally built upon a base laid by Lenin – totalitarianism was what Stalin believed Lenin would have moved to if he had not died. The establishment of the Party Central Committee and the use of the Cheka indicated that Lenin had every intention of centralising control of all aspects of Russian life.

De-Stalinisation

Another power struggle occurred after Stalin's death in 1953. What emerged was a government of collective leadership but one influenced mainly by **Khrushchev**, the Secretary of the Party Central Committee. By 1956 Khrushchev had formulated a plan to move the Soviet Union away from Stalinism. In a speech made in 1956 to the Twentieth Party Congress, Khrushchev denounced Stalin on the grounds that:

- It was not Lenin's wish that Stalin should become leader.
- Stalin had not prepared the Soviet Union adequately for the Second World War.
- Stalin had committed crimes against the Russian people.
- Possible 'outsider' allies, for example Hungary, had been alienated by Stalin.

Khrushchev and his supporters then proceeded with the **de-Stalinisation** of Russia by:

- releasing political prisoners from **Gulags**
- relaxing censorship
- attempting to remove the cult of personality.

However, this did not signal a move away from authoritarian rule. Khrushchev, like previous Russian leaders, continued to use physical force to repress opposition, as was shown by his order to send tanks to Hungary in 1956 to deal with the Nagy regime.

Develop the detail

Below is a sample exam question and a paragraph of an answer to it. The paragraph contains a limited amount of detail. Annotate the paragraph to add additional detail to the answer.

'The introduction of totalitarian rule by Stalin was the only backward step in the development of Russian government from 1855 to 1964.' How far do you agree?

In some ways totalitarian rule was the only backward step. Total control of people's lives was in the hands of one person without any hint of a move towards the representation of the people as had been started by the tsars. Stalin achieved this through repressive measures on a scale not witnessed before. Compared with the tsars, he made much more effective use of propaganda, censorship and the secret police to impose his will. In particular he used these tools of government to implement a range of industrial and agricultural policies designed to enable Russia to compete with the West. The fact that Khrushchev attempted to reverse much of what Stalin had done is evidence that Stalin's period of totalitarian rule was a major backward step. However, in some ways it was not totally backward as Stalin was building on what had already been started by Lenin.

Turning assertion into argument

Below are a sample exam question and a series of assertions. Read the question and then add a justification to each of the assertions to turn it into an argument.

'The introduction of totalitarian rule by Stalin was the most damaging ideology introduced by any Russian ruler from 1855 to 1964.' How far do you agree?

The introduction of totalitarian rule by Stalin was mainly damaging for Russia in the sense that

_____

_____

De-Stalinisation was evidence that Stalin's totalitarianism was considered to have hampered progress in Russia. It showed that Stalin had

_____

_____

However, Stalin's totalitarian approach was not totally damaging as it

_____

_____

Developments in central administration

All Russian leaders during the period from 1855 to 1964 used a centralised form of administration and government. However, the degree of centralisation and the structure of government differed from one ruler to another.

Continuity in central administration

All of the administrations under Russian leaders were hierarchical in nature. At the top was the tsar or, under the communists, the **Politburo**. The various organs of government were always accountable to leaders and not the people. Democracy was debated and experimented with but never fully implemented. The nearest Russia came to achieving democracy fully was through the Provisional Government's efforts in the setting up of the **Constituent Assembly**.

Under all regimes there were numerous organs of government performing specific roles. The tsars used:

- a Council of Ministers, which was the main law-making and administrative body and acted as the main link between other organs of government and the tsar
- the Imperial Council of State, which advised the tsar on legal and financial matters
- a Committee of Ministers, although its responsibilities were divided up in 1906 (see below)
- the Senate, which was the Supreme Court, with its main duty being to act as the final court of appeal on major legal matters.

The communists mainly used:

- the All-Russian Congress of Soviets and the Central Executive Committee (CEC). This was broadly similar to the Council of Ministers used under the tsars. The CEC was, in turn, divided into three political offices: the Politburo, the **Orgburo** and the **Ogburo.**
- the Council of People's Commissars (**Sovnarkom**). Commissars were government ministers who were given specific roles to play; for example, Stalin initially had the job of controlling **national minorities**. In theory, Sovnarkom was answerable only to the CEC.

Change in central administration

Nicholas II responded to the so-called **1905 Revolution** by publishing his October Manifesto. The manifesto led to the abandonment of a Committee of Ministers, with its duties being divided up between:

- the State Council (previously the Imperial Council of State), which was to act as a check on the activity of the *Duma*
- the *Duma* (the elected lower chamber), which was meant to be an assembly of people elected from a range of different social groups.

Nicholas was wary that the *Duma* would not always support his policies so he managed to restrict their power by the passing of the Fundamental Laws of 1906. The laws reinforced the notion that the *Duma* would always be accountable to the tsar. Hence, what appeared on paper to be a major concession to democracy was in reality 'supreme autocratic power' in disguise.

Stalin also implemented a change which appeared to give Russian people throughout the country greater representation. Through his **1936 Constitution**, new representative organs were introduced:

- the Supreme Soviet of the Union of Soviet Socialist Republics (USSR) – the main law-making body
- the Soviet of the Union – which contained representatives of the whole of the USSR
- the Soviet of Nationalities – which represented particular regional groups.

None of this altered the fact that the Communist Party remained, as stated in Article 126 of Stalin's Constitution, 'the nucleus of all the public and state organisations of the working people'. Hence the Supreme Soviet was essentially a puppet of the Communist Party.

Eliminate irrelevance

Below is a sample exam question and a paragraph written in answer to this question. Read the paragraph and identify parts of the paragraph that are not directly relevant to the question. Draw a line through the information that is irrelevant and justify your deletions in the margin.

'Nicholas II's political reforms led to the most important changes in the way Russia was governed from 1855 to 1964.' How far do you agree?

Nicholas II issued his October Manifesto in 1905. The Manifesto outlined his plans for political reform which, most importantly, involved the setting up of an elected *Duma* (a type of parliament). Nicholas also appointed Stolypin as Prime Minister and gave him the brief to change policy on land distribution. The *Duma* met on four occasions before 1914 and was successful in instigating political, economic and social change. However, its powers were severely restricted by the Fundamental Laws of 1906. These laws gave the tsar the authority to close down the *Duma* on a whim, which he did when the first and third *Dumas* appeared too subversive. Thus, when compared with the more permanent political reform of the disbandment of the Constituent Assembly by the Bolsheviks and the introduction of a dictatorship, the creation of the *Duma* cannot be seen as the most important change in the way Russia was governed. Besides, in 1915 Nicholas II allowed a 'progressive bloc' to develop within the *Duma* which demanded that a national government be formed to take charge of the war effort.

Spectrum of importance

Below are a sample exam question and a list of general points which could be used to answer part of the question (the part that would need discussion of how far the administration and structure of Russian central government changed). Use your own knowledge and the information on the opposite page to reach a judgement about the importance of these general points to the question posed.

Write the numbers on the spectrum below to indicate their relative importance. Having done this, write a brief justification of your placement, explaining why some of these factors are more important than others.

'The most important changes in the way Russia was governed from 1855 to 1964 occurred during the rule of Stalin.' How far do you agree?

1   The setting up of Sovnarkom

2   The passing of the Fundamental Laws of 1906

3   The issuing of the Constitution of 1936

4   The use of the Council of Ministers under the tsars

5   The setting up of the *Duma*

6   The planning and establishment of the Constituent Assembly.

Least important   Most important

Changes in local government

Before 1861, provinces were largely under the jurisdiction of noble landowners, and village issues were discussed by the **mir**. The local nobility acted as a bridge between central government and the outreaches of the Empire. This changed with the **emancipation of the serfs**. The nobility ceased to play a political role, and the management of local affairs was left in the hands of local police constables appointed by the Interior Ministry. In 1864 Alexander II also introduced the *Zemstvo* (plural **Zemstva**) or regional council. This was characterised by:

- an elected membership voted in by a mixture of landowners, urban dwellers and peasants. Electors were selected mainly by property qualification.
- locations only in areas considered to be part of **Great Russia**.

In 1870 an urban equivalent was introduced, called the *Duma*. The entry qualification to this body was even tougher than for the *Zemstva* and thus excluded the urban proletariat.

The Third Element

Before October 1917 the *Zemstva* and *Dumas* flourished, providing important services in the fields of education, public health and transport. However, central government increasingly found *Zemstva* members irritating. By the end of the nineteenth century, the councils in some provinces were dominated by teachers, lawyers and doctors who demanded that central government should be remodelled on the lines of the *Zemstva* and *Duma*. This liberal voice was named the 'Third Element'. The other elements were those employed in the 'administration' (government) and those who 'represented the social estates' (nobility).

Both the *Zemstva* and *Duma* (labelled as bourgeois and counter-revolutionary by the Bolsheviks) were abolished after 1917. Local government was then dominated by **soviets**. This situation remained until the end of the period.

Soviets

The first workers' council, or soviet, emerged in St Petersburg at the time of the October Manifesto of 1905. Its aim was to co-ordinate strikes and protect factory workers. Fairly quickly, **Social Revolutionaries (SRs)** and **Social Democrats (SDs)** looked to gain representation on the executive committee and influence how the council was run. In 1917 the council was officially referred to as the **Petrograd Soviet of Workers' Deputies**, and the Bolsheviks began to dominate the executive committee.

The power of the Soviet

From March to October 1917, some historians have claimed the Soviet controlled Russia. It dictated when, where and how strikes would occur. Essential services, especially those connected with transport, were largely in the hands of the Soviet. Petrograd Soviet Order No. 1 placed ultimate authority over soldiers in the hands of the Soviet.

Judicial changes

The judiciary was an important organ of government. However, despite some reforms, the Russian legal system remained archaic compared with that of the West. The main changes were as follows:

- 1864 legal reforms: the introduction of a jury system for criminal cases; the creation of a hierarchy of courts to cater for different types of case; better pay for judges (lessening the chances of corruption); public attendance at courts was allowed.
- 1877: following an assassination attempt on Alexander II's life, a new department of the Senate was set up to try political cases. The **Vera Zasulich case** and the eventual murder of the tsar in 1881 indicated that the new policies of the Senate failed.
- 1881: Alexander III moved away from the 'liberal' approach to law and order that had been adopted by his father. The police were centralised under the Minister for the Interior, special courts were designed for political cases, and Justices of the Peace were replaced by **Land Captains**.
- 1917 onwards: the period of communist rule was dominated by the idea of 'revolutionary justice'. This was epitomised by the new criminal code of 1921 that legalised the use of terror to deter crime (that is, all anti-revolutionary behaviour). The whole judicial system rested on this principle to the end of the period in question.

Identify the concept
a

Below are five sample exam questions based on some of the following concepts:

- **Cause** – questions concern the reasons for something, or why something happened
- **Consequence** – questions concern the impact of an event, an action or a policy
- **Change/continuity** – questions ask you to investigate the extent to which things changed or stayed the same
- **Similarity/difference** – questions ask you to investigate the extent to which two events, actions or policies were similar
- **Significance** – questions concern the importance of an event, an action or a policy.

Read each of the questions and work out which of the concepts they are based on.

'The creation of the *Zemstva* was the most important development in local government in Russia in the period from 1855 to 1964.' How far do you agree?

To what extent did the importance attached to local government change in the period from 1855 to 1964?

'The tsars did more to develop local government than the communists.' How far do you agree?

'Developments in local government in Russia from 1855 to 1964 all stemmed from the reforms of Alexander II.' How far do you agree?

'The nature of local government under the tsars and communists was identical.' How far do you agree?

Identify key terms

Below is a sample question which includes a key word or term. Key terms are important because their meaning can be helpful in structuring your answer, developing an argument, and establishing criteria that will help form the basis of a judgement.

'The most important development in local government in Russia from 1855 to 1964 was changes to the judiciary.' How far do you agree?

- First, identify the key word or term. This will be a word or phrase that is important to the meaning of the question. Underline the word or phrase.
- Secondly, define the key phrase. Your definition should set out the key features of the phrase or word that you are defining.
- Third, make an essay plan that reflects your definition.
- Finally, write a sentence answering the question that refers back to the definition.

Now repeat the task, and consider how the change in key terms affects the structure, argument and final judgement of your essay.

'The effectiveness of local government in Russia from 1855 to 1964 was dependent on changes to the judiciary.' How far do you agree?

Methods of repression and enforcement

The tsars and communists all used repressive measures to enforce policies and restrict opposition. They did this mainly through the use of the secret police, the army, propaganda and censorship. Although there was commonality in the use of repression, historians often emphasise that the communists differed from the tsars in that they used extreme repressive measures purposely to create terror.

The secret police

- Alexander II initially used the Third Section (of the Imperial Chancellery) to exile opponents. He replaced it with the Okhrana in 1880, a less openly aggressive body. The Okhrana was used to target specific individuals and small, rather than large, groups of dissidents. Even though many political opponents were imprisoned or exiled, the secret police was not as effective as it might have been, as is witnessed by the numerous attempts on the life of Alexander II and his assassination in 1881.
- Alexander III and Nicholas II also used the Okhrana, especially against the SRs and SDs.
- The Okhrana lasted until the February Revolution of 1917. The Provisional Government did not want to continue with an institution that had clearly been hated by the Russian people.
- Lenin established the Cheka in December 1917 to deal with those who opposed the Bolshevik seizure of power in October. It became integral to the implementation of War Communism and the **Red Terror** during the Civil War (1917–21).
- Once the Cheka had served its purpose it was replaced by the less brutal United State Police Administration (**OGPU**) in 1924. When Stalin perceived an increase in dissidence towards his personalised form of rule, he introduced the People's Commissariat for Internal Affairs (**NKVD**) in 1934. This marked a return to the days of the Cheka – the NKVD was relentless in clamping down on opposition through **show trials** and **purges**.
- Khrushchev introduced a clearer structure of policing that resulted in the **MVD** being responsible for 'ordinary' criminal acts and civil disorder and the **KGB** being used for internal and external security matters.

The army

- The tsars used the army mainly to quell rebellion and strikes. Alexander III used troops to enforce Russification and Nicholas II consistently used the army to control workers' protests.
- The Military Revolutionary Committee (MRC), a body of soldiers mainly from Petrograd, was encouraged by the Bolsheviks to become the vanguard of the October Revolution. The MRC merged with the **Red Guard** to form the core of Trotsky's **Red Army**. The Red Army was essential to the winning of the Civil War for the Bolsheviks.
- Stalin continued to use the Red Army – it was utilised, like the Cheka, to requisition grain but also to administer the purges.

Propaganda

- Nicholas II used portraits, pamphleteering, photographs and events (for example, the tercentenary celebrations of 300 years of Romanov rule in 1913) to increase his popularity, especially after 1905.
- The communists were the masters of propaganda. They introduced slogans, developed the cult of personality, published party newspapers and promoted 'movements' (for example, the **Stakhanovite movement**) to bolster support for their rule.

Censorship

The tsars and the communists controlled the number of publications in print as well as what was written. Control became very rigid under the communists with the establishment of **Agitprop**, the Association of Proletarian Writers, and 'official' newspapers (*Pravda, Izvestiya* and *Trud*).

Simple essay style

Below is a sample exam question. Use your own knowledge, information on the opposite page and information from other parts of this section on the nature of Russian government to produce a plan for this question. Choose four general points and provide three pieces of specific information to support each general point.

Once you have planned your essay, write the introduction and conclusion for the essay. The introduction should list the points to be discussed in the essay. The conclusion should summarise the key points and justify which point was the most important.

> To what extent were the communists (from 1917 to 1964) more repressive than the tsars (from 1855 to 1917) when implementing their policies?

 Complete the paragraph

Below is a sample exam question and a paragraph of an answer to it. The paragraph lacks a clear point at the start but does contain supporting material and an explanatory link back to the question at the end. Complete the paragraph by writing in the key point at the start. Use the space provided.

> To what extent were the communists more effective than the tsars in their use of repressive measures to govern Russia from 1855 to 1964?

_____

_____

This point is supported by the fact that under the tsars the Third Section followed by the Okhrana were used mainly to target specific individuals and small rather than large groups of dissidents. Even though many political opponents were imprisoned or exiled, the secret police was not as effective as it might have been, as is witnessed by the numerous attempts on the life of Alexander II and his assassination in 1881. In comparison, the communists used the Cheka and, later, the NKVD to seek out large numbers of people who were deemed to oppose any of their policies. In fact, the Cheka was especially brutal in helping Lenin impose War Communism (especially grain requisitioning) on millions of Russians who offered the slightest resistance. Although there was something of a thaw in the intensity of how the secret police was used under Khrushchev, the communists in general did use this institution on a bigger scale to create 'terror' than did the tsars.

The extent and impact of reform

It is important to note that although reforms were often made to improve situations, this was not always the case. For example, War Communism represented reform but it did not equate with an improvement in the lives of the Russian people.

Extent of reform

- It is fair to say that all Russian leaders aimed to industrialise Russia to boost economic growth and to compete with the West.
- Alexander II was notable for promoting railway construction, as was Witte (Finance Minister under Alexander III) during the '**Great Spurt**'. But it was the communists who showed how economic reforms could be used to centralise control over the lives of the people. Nationalisation through the Supreme Economic Council, War Communism, the New Economic Policy (NEP) and the Five-Year Plans were all ways of getting Russians to toe the party line.
- There were also widespread changes in agriculture. The tsars carried out some land reforms starting with the emancipation of the serfs in 1861 (see page 16) and ending with changes made by Stolypin as Russian Prime Minister from 1906 to 1911. In between, Alexander III introduced Land Captains in 1889 to monitor peasant activity. The communists made radical changes, especially through collectivisation.
- All Russian leaders made social reforms to a greater or lesser extent. Most attempted to expand educational provision at all levels as it was increasingly evident that a more educated workforce would mean greater prosperity. Less concern, though, was shown over health provision and housing. By 1955 most citizens were living in accommodation considered to be substandard compared to that in the West. However, Khrushchev did manage to double the housing stock (see page 38).
- Political reforms were also evident throughout the period. The 1861 emancipation edict necessitated changes to local government, hence the introduction of the *Dumas* and *Zemstva*. Prompted by the impact of the Russo-Japanese War (1904–05) and **Bloody Sunday,** Nicholas II brought in a national *Duma*. The Provisional Government (March–October 1917) attempted to continue the path towards democracy by planning for a Constituent Assembly to be put in place. Dramatic political changes then occurred when the Bolsheviks seized power (in October 1917) and created a one-party state.

Stolypin reform

The Stolypin reform (or '**wager on the strong**' as it was sometimes called) involved the following:

- Unused or poorly utilised land was made available to the Peasant Land Bank (established in 1883); peasants could then buy the land from the bank on favourable terms.
- Peasants who were still farming strips (small plots spread over two to three fields) due to the strength of the *mir* were given the right to consolidate their land into smallholdings (small farm units).

In reality, the plan backfired due to the following reasons:

- The process led to an expansion in the numbers joining the wealthier class of peasants who in theory would be more loyal to the tsar. However, they were not totally satisfied as they believed that the best land was still inaccessible to peasants.
- By 1914, about 2 million peasants left the village communes, leaving some regions very short of rural labour. The First World War accelerated this trend. This exodus added to the challenge of keeping supplies of food going to the growing urban population.

Impact of reform

Reforms impacted on different groups, located in different parts of the Empire, at different times.

- Peasants were generally abused and/or neglected throughout the period, although from 1861 onwards they were no longer serfs. Peasants were always those hardest hit by the numerous famines.
- Workers were also exploited by all rulers but in theory were highly valued by the Bolsheviks (and would supposedly go on to create a dictatorship of the proletariat). From the end of 1917 there was improvement with respect to a shortening of working hours, the introduction of a workers' insurance system and bonus schemes but, overall, the impression is that the proletariat were treated in a similar way to peasants.

(!) Spot the mistake ⓐ

Below is a sample exam question and a paragraph written in answer to it. Why does this paragraph not get into at least Level 5? Once you have identified the mistake, rewrite the paragraph so that it displays the qualities of at least Level 5. The mark scheme on page 7 will help you.

'Russian rulers carried out reforms only to control the behaviour of opposition from 1855 to 1964.' How far do you agree?

> Alexander II tried to industrialise as he thought this would help Russia compete with the West. Alexander III appointed Witte to ensure that industrialisation continued. Nicholas II continued to use Witte and a 'Great Spurt' in economic growth occurred as a consequence. Trotsky introduced his New Economic Policy and Stalin introduced his Seven-Year Plans — both leaders developed these ideas to boost the prosperity of Russia and to make it modern. Therefore, it is clear that Russian rulers did not carry out industrial and economic reforms only to control the behaviour of opposition.

(!) Delete as applicable ⓐ

Below is a sample exam question and a paragraph written in answer to it. Read the paragraph and decide which of the possible options (in bold) is more appropriate. Delete the less appropriate options and complete the paragraph by justifying your selection. You will need to use your own knowledge and the text on the opposite page.

To what extent did the tsars (from 1855 to 1917) use reforms more effectively than the communists (from 1917 to 1964) to control opposition?

> The tsars were **sometimes/always** effective in using reforms to control the behaviour of opposition. Alexander II emancipated the serfs in 1861, as he believed that if he failed to do so the Romanov dynasty would be overthrown by **worker/peasant** opposition groups. Alexander III **sometimes/always** used reforms to quell possible unrest, as was shown by his introduction of the Land Captains in 1889. Nicholas II, to a **lesser/greater** extent, also carried out political reforms to appease his opponents. After the **success/debacle** of the Russo-Japanese War and the protests leading to Bloody Sunday, Nicholas **disbanded/introduced** the Duma. By bringing an element of democracy and representation into Russian government, Nicholas hoped to **increase/prevent** demands for a **partial/complete** watering down of **democratic/autocratic** rule.
>
> _____
>
> _____

The nature, extent and effectiveness of opposition before 1917

REVISED

The nature of opposition before 1917

- Before 1917 some very important parties emerged, most notably the **Populists** (Narodniks), Land and Liberty (1876), the **People's Will** (1879), the SDs (1898), SRs (1901), the **Kadets** (1905) and the **Octobrists** (1905).
- Some influential opposition leaders also appeared including **Plekhanov** (SD), Lenin (SD/Bolshevik), **Struve** (Liberal) and **Milyukov** (Kadet).
- Significant peasant protests, in the form of riots, occurred in the early 1860s, 1890s and particularly in 1906 and 1907. They were invariably prompted by dissatisfaction with land allocations, **redemption payments** and food shortages.
- As an urban proletariat grew and became more 'politically conscious', so did its propensity to go on strike and attend protest meetings. For example, there was a wave of sympathy strikes after Bloody Sunday (1905) and a strike at the Lena goldfields in 1912. The most famous strike was probably at the Putilov works in St Petersburg in February 1917 – this is commonly seen as marking the start of the February Revolution.
- The aim of a number of national minority groups was to break away from centralised rule. There were strong nationalist movements in Poland, Finland and parts of the Caucasus region. In other areas, most notably the Baltic provinces, minorities proved to be more compliant. The most passive were Jewish people, mainly because they had no 'homeland' within the Empire.

The effectiveness of opposition before 1917

- More radical opponents of the tsars wanted to see an end to the Romanov dynasty and the implementation of a republic. In this respect, the People's Will was partly successful as it managed to assassinate Alexander II in 1881. Due to radical opposition in the form of the Bolsheviks, the dynasty finally came to an end with the abdication and then murder of Nicholas II in 1918.
- Peasant activists before 1917 wanted greater freedoms, rights to the land and protection against famines. The Emancipation Edict of 1861, the setting up of the *Zemstva* and Stolypin's 'wager on the strong' appeared favourable to peasants. However, such gains must be compared with losses in the form of redemption payments, continued restrictions imposed by the *mir,* poor distribution of land and control over peasant affairs by Land Captains (from 1889 onwards). Famine also continued to be problematic, as demonstrated by the devastating food shortages of 1891. Lenin later tried to win over peasant support by offering 'Peace, Bread and Land'.
- Workers' protests achieved little before 1914. Strikes were put down with considerable force – for example, over 200 workers were killed by the army during the Lena goldfields strike of 1912. Also, there was no factory inspectorate until 1881 to check on working conditions and a ten-hour day was not the norm until the start of the First World War.
- Some national minorities were successful in gaining greater degrees of independence and representation. Finland was actually granted full autonomy in 1905 (although this was quickly reneged on by Stolypin) and Polish National Democratic Party members gained seats in the first and second *Dumas.*

ⓘ Spider diagram

Use the information on the opposite page, page 24 and your own knowledge to add detail to the spider diagram below to assess the reasons why some opponents were more successful than others in challenging the policies of Russian rulers from 1855 to 1964.

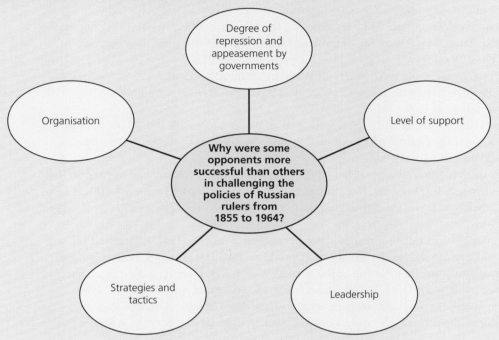

ⓘ Introducing and concluding an argument

Below are a sample exam question, a list of key points to be made in the essay and a simple introduction and conclusion for the essay. Read the question, the key points, the introduction and the conclusion. Use the information on the opposite page and page 24 and your own knowledge to rewrite the introduction and the conclusion in order to develop an argument.

Assess the reasons for some opposition groups being more effective than others in challenging the policies of Russian rulers from 1855 to 1964.

Key points:

- Strategy and tactics – for example, violence
- Strong leadership – for example, Bolsheviks and Lenin
- Importance to the economy – for example, proletariat
- Geographical location – for example, the Poles
- Context – for example, war.

Introduction

There were many reasons why some opposition groups were more successful than others in challenging the policies of Russian rulers from 1855 to 1964. These reasons were linked to strategy and tactics, leadership, the importance to the economy and the geographical location of opposition. It is also important to consider the context within which opposition was operating. Finally, the strengths of each leader need to be discussed. All of these factors help explain why some opposition groups were more effective than others.

Conclusion

To conclude, there were many reasons why some opposition groups were more effective than others in challenging the policies of Russian rulers from 1855 to 1964. These reasons were linked to strategy and tactics, leadership, the importance to the economy and the geographical location of opposition. The context within which opposition was operating was also significant. However, the most important reason was that some leaders were more effective than others in dealing with opposition.

The nature, extent and effectiveness of opposition after 1917

The extent of opposition after 1917

- As opponents to the tsar, the Provisional Government and other political parties, the Bolsheviks were obviously successful in becoming the sole rulers of Russia by 1918. They were also triumphant in taking Russia out of the First World War and defeating their enemies during the Civil War.
- 'Moderate' opponents to the Civil War, and War Communism in particular, emerged within the Bolsheviks. Lenin maintained party unity by appeasing moderates through the introduction of the NEP.
- During the period of rule by Stalin opposition was largely unsuccessful. Purges, show trials and the creation of the **Great Terror** put paid to any opposition from dissident communists, peasants, workers and national minorities.
- Khrushchev introduced de-Stalinisation, which resulted in greater tolerance of opposition. By 1959 there were just 11,000 counter-revolutionaries in Gulags compared with 5.5 million in 1953. Nevertheless, it remained difficult for those who disagreed with Khrushchev's policies to do so effectively.
- National minorities had mixed fortunes in achieving their aims after 1917. Poland and Finland gained full independence after the **Treaty of Brest-Litovsk** (1918) although Poland reverted to being a **satellite state** after the end of the Second World War. Georgia gained temporary independence in 1920 and the Ukraine made, in theory, important gains under the 1936 constitution. Jewish people had been kept in an artificial place of settlement (the Pale of Settlement) since the time of Alexander II and continued to be treated harshly, as shown by the establishment of further 'special' settlements and the **Doctors' Plot** of 1952. This involved the execution of 15 Jewish leaders who had been accused of being subversive.

The effectiveness of opposition after 1917

- The strongest party in existence after 1917 was the Bolshevik Party, which transformed into the Communist Party of the Soviet Union (CPSU) in 1918. The one-party state was reinforced by the Ban on Factions of 1921 – in essence, a ban on any other parties and groups that defied the will of the Communist Party leadership.
- The Civil War (1917–22) saw the greatest opposition to the communists, in the shape of the Whites and **Greens**. The Poles also successfully challenged the Red Army during this period.
- Despite the Ban on Factions, in-fighting continued. It came to a head after Lenin's death, in the form of a power struggle. Stalin successfully dealt with the United Opposition (Trotsky, Kamenev and Zinoviev). This marked the beginning of purges of 'inside' opposition that lasted until the Second World War.
- Peasants opposed War Communism and collectivisation but peasant revolts were ruthlessly put down by the communists. Wealthier peasants, or **kulaks**, became a particular target.
- Workers were generally less prone to oppose the communists although, as shown by the Novocherkassk protests of 1962 (worker protests against food shortages and rising food prices), they would still rebel if they felt they were unjustly treated.
- There was less opposition from national minorities after 1918. This was mainly a result of the 1918, 1924 and 1936 Constitutions but also due to increased repression.

ℹ You're the examiner   a

Below is a sample exam question and a paragraph written in answer to this question. Read the paragraph and the mark scheme provided on page 7. Decide which level you would award the paragraph. Write the level below, along with a justification for your decision.

'Opposition was more successful in achieving its aims under the tsars than under the communists in the period from 1855 to 1964.' How far do you agree?

> Peasant opposition under the tsars aimed to gain personal freedoms for all peasants, a fair allocation of land and regular supplies of food. Peasants were partly successful insofar as Alexander II passed the Emancipation Edict of 1861 which freed peasants from state and noble ownership. The positive effects of this measure were somewhat negated by the stipulation that redemption payments had to be made at high interest rates and the fact that allocations of personal plots of land were deemed inadequate. However, under the instructions of Nicholas II, Stolypin bowed to peasant demands by establishing the 'wager on the strong'. Under this policy, peasants were able to consolidate strips of land into farm units and free themselves from the control of the mir. A Peasant Land Bank was established in 1883 which enabled forward-looking peasants to buy land on favourable terms. Despite some intrusions into peasant life by Land Captains, introduced by Alexander III, by 1900 peasant activists seemed largely content with the improvements that had occurred.

Level: ☐

Reason for choosing this level:

_____

_____

ℹ Establish criteria

Below is a sample exam question which requires you to make a judgement. The key term in the question has been underlined. Defining the meaning of the key term can help you establish criteria that you can use to make a judgement.

Read the question, define the key term and then set out two or three criteria based on the key term, which you can use to reach and justify a judgement.

'The greatest threat to Russian rulers in the period from 1855 to 1964 came from workers' groups.' How far do you agree?

Definition:

_____

Criteria to judge which form of opposition provided the greatest threat to Russian rulers from 1855 to 1964:

_____

_____

_____

_____

Attitudes of the tsars, Provisional Government and communists towards political change

The attitudes of Russian leaders to political change

All the tsars showed a desire to maintain autocracy. Some attempts were made to introduce elements of democracy.

- Alexander II introduced the *Zemstva*.
- Nicholas II introduced the national *Duma*.

In both instances the changes were made alongside efforts to maintain tsarist rule. The *Zemstva* proved to be unrepresentative of the population as a whole and the *Duma* had its powers limited by the Fundamental Law of 1906.

The Provisional Government had a more positive attitude towards political change in aiming to set up a Constituent Assembly. The principles upon which the achievement of this aim depended also led to political change of a more liberal nature. These included:

- the release of political prisoners
- the formation of an alliance with the Petrograd Soviet.

The communists initially wanted revolutionary political change. As a result, the tsar was forced to abdicate, the Provisional Government was constantly challenged and the Constituent Assembly was disbanded. Once the October Revolution was over the communists were more interested in consolidating power using the political system they had created. Although constitutions were issued that appeared to give greater autonomy to certain regional groups in the Soviet Union, under Stalin power became more centralised. Stalin seemed intent on introducing totalitarianism using tools of extreme repression to do so. Khrushchev showed a greater willingness to embrace political change by de-Stalinising Russia and shifting authority to the Party.

The extent of political change

Under the tsars the ideology and structure of government largely stayed the same. Leaders made some changes but they were always subservient to the need to maintain autocracy. All of the tsars used a mixture of reform and repression to govern and to keep opposition under control. Thus, to label Alexander II the 'Liberator' and Alexander III the 'Reactionary' is misleading.

The Provisional Government's principles that guided the establishment of the Constituent Assembly contributed to its downfall. For example, releasing political prisoners allowed opposition groups to gather momentum. Also, the Constituent Assembly was short-lived and was replaced in dramatic fashion by a Bolshevik dictatorship.

Political change under Lenin and Stalin mainly came about through the constitutions of 1924 and 1936. These extended the range of influence over a number of republics, but also suggested that each member state would have a degree of autonomy. A more marked change occurred with de-Stalinisation and a move back to a form of democratic centralism.

Support your judgement

Below are a sample exam question and two basic judgements. Read the exam question and the two judgements. Support the judgement that you agree with more strongly by adding a reason that justifies the judgement.

'The communists (from 1917 to 1964) were more willing and able to implement political change than the tsars (from 1855 to 1917).' How far do you agree?

> Overall, communist leaders were far more willing and able than the tsars in implementing political change.
>
> _____
>
> _____

> The tsars were as able but were far less willing than the communist leaders when it came to implementing political change.
>
> _____
>
> _____

Tip: Whichever option you choose, you will have to weigh up both sides of the argument. You could use words like 'although' and 'whereas' in order to help the process of evaluation.

Recommended reading

Below is a list of suggested further reading on this topic.

- Andrew Holland, *Access to History: Russia and its Rulers 1855–1964* (2016)
- Michael Lynch, *Access to History: Reaction and Revolution: Russia 1894–1924* (third edition, 2005)
- Robert Service, *A History of Modern Russia From Nicholas II to Putin* (2003)
- Peter Waldron, *The End of Imperial Russia, 1855–1917* (1997)
- Hugh Seton-Watson, *The Russian Empire 1801–1917* (1967)
- J. N. Westwood, *Endurance and Endeavour: Russian History 1812–2001* (fifth edition, 2002)

Exam focus

Below is a sample high-level essay. Read the response and the comments around it.

'The communist leaders were more effective autocrats than the tsars in governing Russia from 1855 to 1964.' How far do you agree?

An autocrat is a ruler with absolute authority. An effective autocrat is one who maintains absolute authority and stability through adapting the organs and tools of government, balancing this against the introduction of progressive reforms. In this sense, some communists were more effective than the tsars as autocratic leaders but much depended on their circumstances.

> The candidate starts by offering a clear definition of what might constitute an 'effective autocrat'. There is a good indication here of how the rest of the answer is likely to be structured and argued.

When Alexander II came to rule he evidently intended to continue with his father's approach, which was epitomised by the slogan 'Orthodoxy, Authority and Nationality'. Although Alexander became known as a great reformer (the 'Liberator') he continued to promote autocracy as a way of ruling sanctioned by God. Alexander III, mainly through the use of force, and Nicholas II, through a mixture of force and propaganda, were also successful in promoting autocracy as the only and best way to rule. The communists also adopted autocracy but twisted it to suit their particular ideologies. Lenin justified his Marxism–Leninism-based dictatorship by arguing it was a necessary short-term step before the proletariat could govern Russia themselves. He believed this would lead to a more egalitarian society. Stalin built on this notion and introduced totalitarian rule. As with the tsars, he used repression and propaganda effectively, utilising the cult of personality to get the people to adopt his ideology. Although Khrushchev moved away from the Great Terror of Stalin by de-Stalinising Russia, he continued to rule autocratically. Thus, it is fair to say that the communists and the tsars were equally effective in adopting and promoting autocracy. What differed was the way in which autocracy was interpreted and implemented.

> The candidate has developed the theme of ideology here. There is a consistent focus on how effectively different regimes promoted the ideology of autocracy. The candidate has also synthesised material by linking and comparing the approaches used by the tsars and communists.

The structure of government under the tsars continued in a form that fitted with autocracy. All of the main institutions of government were answerable to the tsar. The Council of Ministers, the Imperial Council of State, the Committee of Ministers, the Senate and the Supreme Court were all controlled directly or indirectly by the tsar. Following significant changes with the introduction of the *Duma* in 1905, the tsar was consistent in ensuring that he maintained sole authority. Nicholas II introduced the Fundamental Laws of 1906 to clarify that 'No new law can be legally binding without the approval of the Sovereign Emperor'. The fact that Nicholas was able to disband the first two sittings of the *Duma* with ease illustrates his effectiveness as an autocrat. A similar pattern occurs with respect to the *Zemstva*, which had been introduced by Alexander II. As the local councils gained what was considered to be too much power they were reined in through the introduction of Land Captains (1889). The communists were probably even more effective at using a structured administration to maintain autocratic rule. They moved away from any semblance of democracy and introduced a centralised structure of government dominated by Lenin and leading Bolsheviks. Lenin used the All-Russian Congress of Soviets, the Central Executive Committee (CEC) and the Council of People's Commissars (Sovnarkom) to govern – but *Sovnarkom* had to obey the CEC, which in turn was dominated by Lenin and close advisers. Stalin used a similar approach and similar institutions, although his 1936 constitution theoretically gave some increased representation to national minorities.

> The candidate has used a good level of knowledge and understanding of the structure of government to show how autocracy was implemented. The structure of government is an area of the specification that candidates often neglect.

All of the tsars used repression to maintain autocracy. The secret police, in the form of the Third Section and then the Okhrana (1880), were especially adept at rooting out dissidents and having them either imprisoned, exiled or executed. However, there were numerous assassination attempts against Alexander II and eventually he lost his life to the People's Will in 1881. Nicholas II was also ineffective in preventing the proliferation of opposition groups so that a Socialist Democratic splinter group, the Bolsheviks, eventually seized power and murdered the tsar and his family. The communists were better at using the secret police than the tsars. Lenin used the Cheka to implement War Communism and to win the Civil War. Stalin used the NKVD to eradicate opposition and to terrorise the population to an extent that they would never dream of challenging his authority. Khrushchev also used the secret police (MVD and KGB) to maintain autocratic rule but his move away from terrorising the people possibly led to his downfall in 1964.

The tsars and communists also used the army, censorship and propaganda to rule autocratically. The tsars used the army mainly to quell rebellion and strikes. Alexander III used troops to enforce Russification and Nicholas II consistently used the army to control workers' protests. Under the communists the army was used differently but not necessarily more effectively to maintain autocracy. The Red Army was essential to the winning of the Civil War for the Bolsheviks. Stalin continued to use the Red Army, as with the Cheka, to requisition grain but also to administer the purges. Nicholas II used portraits, pamphleteering, photographs and events as propaganda to increase his popularity, especially after 1905. However, the communists were the masters of propaganda. They introduced slogans, developed the cult of personality, published party newspapers and promoted 'movements' (for example, the Stakhanovite movement) to bolster support for their rule. The tsars and the communists controlled the number of publications in print as well as what was written. Control became very rigid under the communists with the establishment of Agitprop, the Association of Proletarian Writers and 'official' newspapers (*Pravda, Izvestiya* and *Trud*). These institutions were especially effective in preventing the spread of anti-Stalinist ideas.

Finally, economic reforms were used by the tsars and communists to govern autocratically. It could be argued that the economic reforms of the tsars as characterised, for example, by the Great Spurt were done partly in response to the disastrous effects of wars but also to improve the living standards of the population. In theory, this would have subsequently led to greater support for the tsar. Similarly, Lenin introduced the New Economic Policy to appease some supporters. The fact that under each tsar, peasant and worker unrest mounted, whereas it was non-existent under the communists, suggests that the economic policies of the latter were more effective. With respect to social reform the tsars were also less effective.

In conclusion, the tsars and communists were both effective in maintaining autocracy but the degree of effectiveness differed according to circumstance and the methods used. The eventual downfall of the Romanov dynasty suggests that overall the tsars were less effective autocrats. However, to become more effective autocrats, the communists, especially Stalin, had to use levels of repression never witnessed before in Russia.

The candidate has continued to write thematically and has thus avoided a chronological, narrative-based answer. This approach undoubtedly leads to marks in the higher levels of the mark scheme. However, there is a bit of a drift here to listing/describing how the secret police were used rather than discussing how effectively they were used.

This candidate has done well here to condense material down into a manageable chunk while maintaining relevance. Again, there is a slight tendency to list developments but, given the parameters that the candidate has had to work to, this is understandable.

The candidate has made a good attempt to continue to write synoptically. A good awareness of how economic reforms were used as tools of government is displayed. If time had permitted, maybe the candidate could have used a bit more evidence to support some of the observations.

The candidate has written a short but pointed conclusion. A clear judgement is made although it is not totally convincing in that the main body of the essay does not always explicitly deal with the issue of 'circumstance'.

The essay includes accurate and relevant evidence and a range of appropriate historical terminology. It is clearly structured and coherent. The candidate shows a very good understanding of key concepts, especially change and continuity over time. The answer retains focus and displays an analytical approach. Generally, there is very good synthesis and the essay finishes with a sound judgement. There is a little bit of drift towards description and assertion which detracts from the overall quality.

2 The impact of dictatorial regimes on the economy and society of the Russian Empire and the USSR

Reasons for and extent of economic change

REVISED

Reasons for economic change

The main reasons for changes were:

- Throughout the period 1855 to 1964, Russian leaders were keen to accelerate industrialisation to create a wealthier Russia, although there was a consistent emphasis on heavy (iron, steel, coal and engineering) as opposed to light industry.
- This was connected to the main motive for industrialising, which was to 'catch up with the West'. The great Western powers, especially Britain, France and Germany (especially after 1871), had seemingly based their economic progress on the development of the iron and coal industries.
- Russian leaders sought to emulate the industrial revolutions that had occurred in these countries – they believed this was the obvious way to increase and maintain Russia's military status at a time when global power struggles were becoming more prevalent.

Extent of economic change

Although at the start of the period progress was slow, economic change under the tsars was generally extensive. During the period 1909 to 1913 industrial output increased on average by 7 per cent per year and GNP by 3.5 per cent per year. This at least matched the performance of many other nations, although not Russia's main competitors. For example, by 1913 Russian coal production was 10 per cent that of Britain and GNP per capita only 20 per cent that of Britain.

Under the communists, particularly Stalin, there was a more substantial increase in the rate of growth of GNP. The average annual rate before 1940 was between 5 and 6 per cent. Most of this extra wealth came from four key industries: coal, steel, oil and electricity. However, although the growth rates were at times higher than those being achieved in the West, the 'extra' wealth was not necessarily passed on to the bulk of the population. Also, such economic success was achieved at great human cost – up to 3.4 million people were forced to work in labour camps, under appalling conditions, to achieve production targets for certain industries.

Economic change under the tsars and communists was stimulated mainly by key developments in industry and agriculture, summarised in the table below. Note that Russian leaders generally thought that agriculture was important because of the way that it served industry. Industrial workers could not produce their own food and therefore increasingly relied on the efforts of peasants to provide food for them.

Rulers	Industry	Agriculture
The tsars	The Reutern reforms (1862–78) – encouragement of foreign investment and foreign technical expertise	The emancipation of the serfs (1861)
		The Peasant Land Bank (1883)
	Railway construction – the Trans-Siberian line	The Stolypin reforms (1906–1911) – the 'wager on the strong' and land reforms
	The **Medele'ev tariff** (1891) – raised government revenues	
		The emergence of kulaks and commercial farming
	The Witte reforms (1893–1903) – the 'Great Spurt'	
The communists	State Capitalism – central control of the economy through the Supreme Economic Council (December 1917)	Collectivisation and **dekulakisation** (1929 onwards) – the *kolkhozy*, the *sovkhozy* and the coming of motor-tractor stations (MTS). MTS were responsible for loaning tractors to peasants, distributing seed, collecting grain and deciding what farmers could keep for their own consumption
	War Communism – nationalisation, partial militarisation of labour and **grain requisitioning**	
	The NEP – denationalisation of small-scale enterprise and a return to private ownership	
	Centralised planning – the seven Five-Year Plans under Stalin and Khrushchev and the aim of economic **autarky**	The **Virgin Lands scheme** (1954 onwards) – by 1964, 165 million acres had been given over to the production of wheat

Table 2.1 Economic change under the tsars and communists: the key developments in industry and agriculture.

⚠ Spider diagram

Use the information on the opposite page to add detail to the spider diagram below in response to the following question.

Assess the reasons why some Russian rulers were more successful than others in improving the Russian economy from 1855 to 1964.

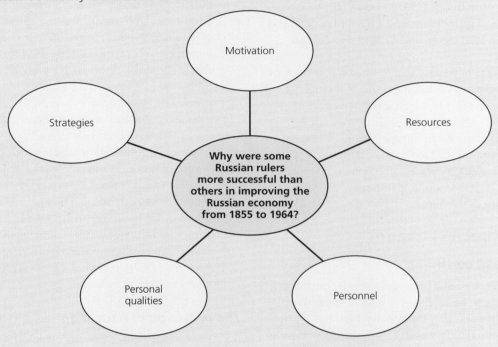

⚡ Spectrum of importance

Below is a sample exam question and a list of general points which could be used to answer the question. Use your own knowledge and the information on the opposite page to reach a judgement about the importance of these general points to the question posed.

Write numbers on the spectrum below to indicate their relative importance. Having done this, write a brief justification of your placement, explaining why some of these factors are more important than others. The resulting diagram could form the basis of an essay plan.

How far do you agree that the most important developments in the industrialisation of Russia, from 1855 to 1964, occurred as a result of the reforms made by Witte?

1 The Reutern reforms (1862–78)

2 The Medele'ev tariff (1891)

3 The Witte reforms (1893–1903)

4 Lenin's State Capitalism, War Communism and the NEP

5 Stalin's Five-Year Plans and the aim of economic autarky

6 Khrushchev's Five-Year Plans.

Least important   Most important

Reasons for social change

The reasons for social change were partly linked to economic change but also to the ideological stance taken by each leader. The most important reasons were:

- Population growth (see below), mostly due to a 'natural rate of growth' (that is, a rising birth rate and a falling death rate) stimulated by better economic conditions.
- Large numbers of peasant families had started to move to towns and cities in search of industrial employment – this led to changes in the stratification or structure of society.
- The nobility declined in numbers by 1914, mainly as a result of having to sell land to pay off debts.
- Communist ideology placed an emphasis on equality and gave a greater amount of authority and responsibility to workers.

Extent of social change

Population growth

The population of Russia grew substantially during the period in question. In 1858 there were 74 million inhabitants of the Russian Empire. By 1960 the population of the USSR was 212 million. These figures obviously need to be viewed in light of the fact that the composition of the Empire and Soviet Union changed significantly over the period.

Social structure

The social structure of Russia changed as follows:

- By the end of the nineteenth century Russian society was still very rural based – about 80 per cent of the population was reliant on agriculture.
- A significant development was the rise of a middle class (essentially industrialists, those involved in commerce and professionals). By 1914 there were probably about 2 million people who fell into the middle-class bracket.
- The nobility was in decline – in the 1870s the gentry owned about 200 million acres of land, but this had fallen to 140 million acres by 1914.
- The social structure underwent a dramatic change when the communists came into power. The majority of society was officially made up of workers, but communist governments were dominated by a hierarchical bureaucracy led by an elite. After a while status rankings even appeared among workers – some were called 'technical experts' and were given privileges. By the early 1930s there were supposedly 1.5 million promotions of ordinary workers to managers.

The provision of education

An area of social change that impacted on social status was education. Important changes occurred in the provision of elementary (primary) and secondary education under the tsars and communists. These changes are summarised in the following table.

Rulers	Elementary	Secondary	Higher Education
The tsars	Alexander II placed the administration of elementary education with the *Zemstva*. By 1877 the Ministry of Education had taken control of elementary provision; school inspectors were introduced. The number of primary schools rose from 23,000 in 1880 to 81,000 in 1914.	Alexander II introduced a 'new code' for secondary schools which resulted in a doubling of the number attending such institutions by 1865. Alexander III reversed his father's policy by banning lower-class children from attending secondary schools.	Under Stolypin all non-academic meetings of students at universities were made illegal. Alexander III took away much of the autonomy of universities.
The communists	In 1930 attendance at primary school was made compulsory to the age of 12. By 1930 there were 18 million children attending primary schools.	The 'bourgeois' gymnasia were scrapped and replaced with polytechnic (vocational) schools. By 1932 there were 6.9 million pupils attending secondary schools. In 1939 Stalin scrapped school fees.	

! Support or challenge?

Below is a sample exam question which asks how far you agree with a specific statement. Below this are a series of general statements which are relevant to the question. Using your own knowledge and the information on the opposite page, decide whether these statements support or challenge the statement in the question and tick the appropriate box.

'Both the tsars and communists were reluctant to make social reforms, especially in education in the period from 1855 to 1964.' How far do you agree with this view?

	SUPPORT	CHALLENGE
Alexander II introduced a 'new code' for secondary schools which resulted in a doubling of the number attending such institutions by 1865.		
By 1877 the Ministry of Education had taken control of elementary provision and school inspectors were introduced to check on standards.		
Alexander III reversed his father's policy by banning lower-class children from attending secondary schools.		
Under Stolypin all non-academic meetings of students at universities were made illegal.		
In 1930 attendance at primary school was made compulsory to the age of 12.		
The 'bourgeois' gymnasia were scrapped by Stalin and replaced with polytechnic (vocational) schools.		
Alexander III took away much of the autonomy of universities.		

! Simple essay style

Below is a sample exam question. Use your own knowledge and the information on the opposite page to produce a plan for this question. Choose four general points and provide three pieces of specific information to support each general point.

Once you have planned your essay, write the introduction and conclusion for the essay. The introduction should list the points to be discussed in the essay. The conclusion should summarise the key points and justify which point was the most important.

'The most important social changes in Russia from 1855 to 1964 concerned educational provision.' How far do you agree?

Changes to rural living and working conditions

Changes to rural living conditions

Peasants constituted the bulk of the Russian population from 1855 to 1964 (from about 90 per cent in 1855 to about 70 per cent by the 1950s). Living conditions for the average peasant remained the same across the period, although there was regional variation and some differences between different 'classes' of peasant especially after Stolypin's 'wager on the strong' was introduced (see page 20).

Rural housing

- The standard peasant house was the *izba*, a single-room wooden hut heated by an oven which also acted as a sleeping platform. Animals as well as families were accommodated in the hut. Conditions were cramped, cold, damp and grubby. On the plus side, the huts were cheap to construct – but generally the living conditions experienced by peasants were very poor.
- Under Stalin there was some change in the way peasants were housed. 'Special' housing blocks were constructed on the periphery of the new collective farms. However, kulaks were often allocated the worst housing in barracks or forced into tented shelter in fields.
- Khrushchev ordered the construction of self-contained '**agro-towns**' for peasants, but again they were built cheaply and quickly and subsequently were of a poor standard.

Changes to rural working conditions

Work on the land was always dictated by 'nature's clock'. Specific jobs could only be completed at certain times of the year. The success of peasant farmers was influenced mostly by the quality of the soil, the weather and their innate ability to farm rather than by government policies.

However, governments did intervene in ways that had a major impact on the way peasants worked. It is fair to say that working conditions for peasants worsened under the communists, as peasants were generally seen as being less important to the future of Russia than the proletariat. Although Lenin and Stalin changed their minds and saw the revolutionary potential of peasants, rural workers were still viewed as being important only as food producers for urban dwellers. The following developments impacted significantly on rural working conditions.

- The Emancipation Edict of 1861 – this was pivotal as, in theory, it freed serfs to work as they wished on their own land. But redemption payments and the continued influence of the *mir* (an institution that lasted until 1930) restricted the activities of peasants.
- Stolypin's 'wager on the strong' (see page 20) from 1906 onwards led to a new class of independent, surplus-producing peasants (kulaks).
- Under War Communism (see page 10) kulaks were accused of grain hoarding. The Cheka was employed to requisition grain and imprison kulaks who were deemed to be against the revolution.
- With the NEP (see page 10) the attitude towards kulaks changed. They were seen as the more 'cultured and educated' peasants but were still persecuted to an extent – they paid higher taxes than other peasants, were disenfranchised and their children were prevented from attending state schools.
- Under Stalin's collectivisation policy (see page 12) the fortunes of peasants changed once more. Kulaks were viewed as incompatible with collectivisation and a policy of dekulakisation was implemented. It is estimated that from the start of 1928 to the end of 1930, 1 to 3 million kulak families (6 to 18 million people) were deported to work camps in places such as Siberia.
- Stalin, similarly to Witte, siphoned off quantities of grain for export and used the resultant capital to finance industry. This meant an even greater strain on supplies made available to peasants and workers.
- Dekulakisation disappeared under Khrushchev, but his Virgin Lands scheme once again put sections of the peasantry under pressure to increase their productivity.

! Spider diagram

Use the information on the opposite page to add detail to the spider diagram below in response to the following question.

To what extent did rural working and living conditions in Russia improve in the period from 1855 to 1964?

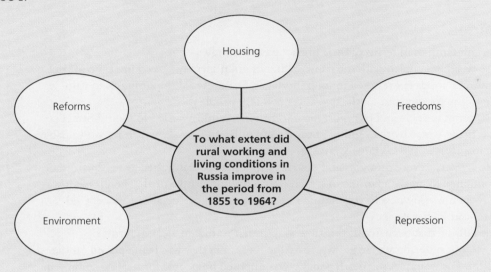

◊ Identify an argument a

Below are a series of definitions, a sample exam question and two sample conclusions. One of the conclusions achieves a high level because it contains an argument (an assertion justified with a reason). The other achieves a lower level because it contains only description (a detailed account) and assertion (a statement of fact or an opinion, which is not supported by a reason). Identify which is which. The mark scheme on page 7 will help you.

'Life for peasants was consistently bleak in the period from 1855 to 1964.' How far do you agree?

There were times when life for peasants was very bleak indeed. This was especially the case with respect to the famines of 1891 and 1932–34 when hundreds of thousands of peasants died. However, there were other times when living and working conditions for peasants improved. The Emancipation Edict of 1861 freed peasants, and Stolypin's 'wager on the strong', to some extent, put right some of the problems that had arisen from emancipation.

Life for peasants was definitely bleak during the period 1855 to 1964, especially when it came to food availability. Obviously, the main task of peasants was to produce food for the Russian peoples and for export. However, increasingly, peasants were put under pressure to produce more for urban dwellers who did not have time to grow their own food. More food was also redistributed away from peasant communities. Throughout the period from 1855 to 1964 there were numerous periods of food shortages or famines that invariably hit the peasants hardest.

Famines

The main task of peasants was to produce food for the Russian peoples and for export. However, increasingly, peasants were put under pressure to produce more for urban dwellers who did not have time to grow their own food. More food was also redistributed away from peasant communities. Between 1855 to 1964 there were numerous periods of food shortages or famines that invariably hit the peasants hardest.

Major famines

The most important famines in terms of their impact were as follows:

- 1891: Adverse weather coupled with the panic selling of grain surpluses to counter the impact of a new consumer goods tax resulted in food shortages. Peasants sold the surpluses to gain extra income to pay for increases in the tax. Over 350,000 people died.
- 1914–18: Disruption to trade and transport during the First World War led to food shortages. The crisis was made worse by the signing of the Treaty of Brest-Litovsk, which meant valuable grain-producing areas in the Ukraine were lost.
- 1921: Terrible winters, severe droughts and destruction of transport infrastructures due to the Civil War combined to create a famine in which over 5 million people died. The problem was made worse by Lenin's slowness in responding to the crisis and his reluctance to accept aid from the American Relief Agency.
- 1932–34: The famine that occurred at this time was similar to that in 1921 in terms of mortality levels, but suffering was made worse by the repression that was being placed on the people by Stalin. For example, the death penalty was imposed on people for stealing grain – in such cases the grain may have been produced and owned by the accused but they were accused of hoarding and therefore stealing from the people.
- In general, the policy of exporting grain, used especially by Witte and Stalin, exacerbated food shortages and contributed to the causes of famines.

Improvement in the 1930s: a turning point?

By 1935 matters seemed to improve and food production increased slowly. However, on the eve of the Second World War it was unlikely that total food output had reached pre-First World War levels. Generally, the diet of workers in particular seemed to worsen under the communists. By the late 1930s, for example, the consumption of meat and fish had fallen by 80 per cent.

The Second World War and food supplies

During the Second World War, the policy towards collectivisation was relaxed. With the removal of restrictions on the size of private plots of land, food production rose. However, this was short-lived, as another famine took place in 1947. The pattern of poor harvests and associated food shortages continued during the rule of Khrushchev. Despite the Virgin Lands campaign and improvements to the state pricing mechanism for agricultural produce, food still had to be imported. Critics – at the time and since – believed that adherence to a policy of subsidised 'socialised agriculture' simply led to inefficiency and a situation whereby the demand for food in Russia always outstripped the ability of Russian farmers to meet it.

⧫ Support your judgement

Below are a sample exam question and two basic judgements. Read the exam question and the two judgements. Support the judgement that you agree with more strongly by adding a reason that justifies the judgement.

'The people of Russia frequently experienced food shortages in the period from 1855 to 1964 as a result of government policies.' How far do you agree?

Overall, the economic policies of most Russian governments across the period did lead to food shortages especially for those living in rural areas.

_____

_____

Generally, food shortages in Russia across the period were the result of natural phenomena such as poor weather; only Stalin's policies could be said to have artificially created famine.

_____

_____

Tip: Whichever option you choose, you will have to weigh up both sides of the argument. You could use words like 'although' and 'whereas' in order to help the process of evaluation.

① Establish criteria

Below is a sample exam question which requires you to make a judgement. The key term in the question has been underlined. Defining the meaning of the key term can help you establish criteria that you can use to make a judgement.

Read the question, define the key term and then set out two or three criteria based on the key term, which you can use to reach and justify a judgement.

'Russian leaders showed <u>minimal concern</u> over food shortages in the period from 1855 to 1964.' How far do you agree?

Definition:

_____

_____

Criteria to judge the extent to which Russian leaders showed minimal concern over food shortages in the period from 1855 to 1964:

_____

_____

_____

_____

Changes to urban living and working conditions

Urbanisation and living conditions

Urbanisation was a slow, gradual process in Russia. It went hand-in-hand with industrialisation, as industries tended to locate near to where there was already a reasonable pool of labour – that is, in the areas around the big cities of St Petersburg and Moscow. With urbanisation came the associated public health problems of overcrowding, substandard housing, inadequate water supplies and poor drainage. The end result was outbreaks of disease such as cholera. Thus, urbanisation created new problems for Russian leaders to confront, in addition to those associated with the more traditional rural-based ways of living.

Urban housing

- By the end of the nineteenth century about 15 per cent of the Russian population lived in towns and cities, compared with 80 per cent in Britain and 40 per cent in the USA. Only 19 cities had more than 100,000 inhabitants. St Petersburg (1.25 million inhabitants) and Moscow (1 million inhabitants) were the largest cities.
- By 1914 there were over 1,000 towns containing, in total, about 2 million buildings. Over 50 per cent of housing was made from wood and therefore prone to fire damage. Most houses and streets were lit by kerosene lamps – only 74 towns had access to electricity and 35 to gas. Around 200 towns had piped water and 38 towns had a sewerage system.
- Disease associated with urbanisation spread rapidly. In 1910, for example, there were over 100,000 deaths from cholera in St Petersburg alone.
- Special workers' housing was built near to industrial cities. These 'barracks' were hastily built and were invariably overcrowded and insanitary.
- The Decree on Land issued by the Bolsheviks in 1917 partly focused on what the party intended to do about housing. Dwellings in towns and cities were to be taken from private owners and handed over to the proletariat under the guidance of the soviets.
- Improvements to housing made by Lenin were reversed by Stalin. The Stalinist policy was to allocate space rather than rooms to individuals and families, especially within the new high-rise tenements. Overcrowding once more became the norm. In Moscow in the mid-1930s, for example, different families often had to share single units of accommodation (one room). The Second World War resulted in 25 million Russians being made homeless. This problem was not really addressed until after Stalin's death in 1953. The housing stock doubled from 1955 to 1964 and the principles of communal living were abandoned. However, the introduction of housing co-operatives tended to favour the professional classes, as they were the only ones who could afford the deposits on new housing.

Urban working conditions

Conditions under the tsars

Town and city workers were employed either in service industries or manufacturing. The worst working conditions were found in factories, mines, iron and steel plants and engineering works. There was no factory inspectorate until 1882 and working conditions for many, especially factory-based textile workers, remained dangerous and unhealthy. Even after inspectors were introduced, there were too few of them and they had limited powers to enforce safety guidelines. Internal passports were a way of controlling migration to urban areas to alleviate some of the issues linked to living and working conditions. In 1917 and 1932, communist leaders revamped and imposed the internal passport system more strictly.

Key changes under the tsars

- 1882: Employment in factories of children under the age of 12 was banned (although note the issue regarding inspectors, mentioned above).
- 1896: An 11-hour working day was fixed by law. Workers were not obliged to work on Sundays.
- 1903: A workers' insurance scheme was introduced (adapted in 1912).
- 1914: Statutory holidays had been introduced by this time and most employers were operating to a nine- to ten-hour working day.

Conditions under the communists

Ironically, working conditions for the proletariat seemed to worsen under the communists, at least in the short term. Generally, hours of work per day were extended (especially under Stalin), pay was relatively low and a 'new work discipline' was enforced harshly. The Stalinist regime imposed heavy fines for breaking work rules (usually ten per cent of wages) and some workers were threatened with being 'purged' if they were found out to be 'wreckers' (those who slowed or disrupted production).

Key changes under Lenin and Stalin

- 1920: Rabkrin (Workers' and Peasants' Inspectorate) was established but proved to be a retrograde step – it simply became a discussion group rather than a law-enforcing body.
- 1932 onwards: Stalin demanded that workers operated to a 10- to 12-hour working day to fulfil the requirements of his Five-Year Plans.
- 1939: As a result of the alleged success of the first Five-Year Plan, the average working day went down to seven hours. Bonus schemes were organised and the Stakhanovite movement was popularised.

! Spot the mistake

Below is a sample exam question and a paragraph written in answer to this question. Why does this paragraph not get into Level 5? Once you have identified the mistake, rewrite the paragraph so that it displays the qualities of Level 5 at least. The mark scheme on page 7 will help you.

To what extent was the working class of Russia failed more by Bolshevik than tsarist rule between 1855 and 1964?

One area of life in which the working class of Russia was failed more by the tsars than the Bolsheviks was housing. By 1914 there were over 1,000 towns containing about 2 million buildings in total. Over 50 per cent of housing was made from wood and therefore prone to fire damage. Most houses and streets were lit by kerosene lamps — only 74 towns had access to electricity and 35 to gas. Around 200 towns had piped water and 38 a sewerage system. The tsars did very little to alleviate these conditions. The peasants experienced disease associated with urbanisation. In 1910, for example, there were over 100,000 peasant deaths from cholera in St Petersburg alone. Special workers' housing was built near to industrial cities. These 'barracks' were hastily built and were invariably overcrowded and insanitary.

! Delete as applicable

Below is a sample exam question and a paragraph written in answer to this question. Read the paragraph and decide which of the possible options (in bold) is most appropriate. Delete the least appropriate options and complete the paragraph by justifying your selection.

To what extent did urban living and working conditions remain uniformly poor from 1855 to 1964?

For **part/most/all** of the period from 1855 to 1964 urban living conditions remained poor. During the **late/middle/early** part of the period **some/many** urban dwellings were overcrowded, which resulted in insanitary conditions and the spread of urban killer diseases such as **arthritis/mumps/cholera**. In 1910, for example, there were over 100,000 deaths from **arthritis/mumps/cholera** in St Petersburg alone. There was **some/a lot of** progress under the Bolsheviks with the issuing of the Decree on Land in 1917. This decree stipulated that dwellings in towns and cities were to be taken from private owners and handed over to the **peasants/proletariat** under the guidance of the **secret police/soviets**. Improvements to housing made by Lenin were **partly/totally** reversed by Stalin. The Stalinist policy was to allocate **space/amenities** rather than rooms to individuals and families, especially within the new high-rise tenements. Overcrowding once more became the norm.

_____

_____

Limitations on personal, political and religious freedom   REVISED

Limitations on personal and political freedom

A common feature of all Russian leaders' periods of rule is that they limited the personal and political freedoms of the masses – that is, the freedom to exercise their power by voting, joining political parties or pressure groups and expressing their views through the media.

Voting

As no representative assembly was established in Russia for any length of time there was never a move towards a **universal franchise**. However, there were times when some groups could vote for bodies that had a brief to represent the views of the people in a rather limited way:

- In 1864 *Zemstva* (regional councils) were set up to express views of rural people at a local level. Members were elected by property qualification and therefore included landowners, some urban dwellers and wealthier peasants only.
- Similarly there were elections to the national *Duma* after 1905, but again the franchise was limited.
- Elections to various bodies did exist under the communists but were highly controlled by the elite in Russian government. For example, under Stalin the Central Committee (of Congress) was a collective body elected at the annual party congress. It was authorised to meet at least twice a year to act as the party's supreme governing body. Membership of the Central Committee increased from 71 full members in 1934 to over 200 by the end of the period.

Political parties and pressure groups

- Although political parties were monitored and controlled to some extent under the tsars they were allowed to exist. Thus, from 1855 to 1917 a number of parties and groups emerged including the Populists, the People's Will, the SRs, the SDs), the Liberals, Kadets and Octobrists. Under the communists, only one political party existed – from March 1918 onwards, the Russian Communist Party dominated Russian political life.
- Before 1905, trade unions were banned. From 1905 to 1917 they were allowed to exist but with very limited powers. Under the communists, trade unions were valued but were always subordinate to the needs of government rather than the needs of the proletariat.

- From 1905 onwards, soviets (workers' councils) appeared and were tolerated. The Provisional Government actually formed a '**Dual Authority**' with the Petrograd Soviet. Soviets were integral to the Bolshevik seizure of power and were integrated into the communist political system after the October Revolution of 1917.

Expression of views through the media

The tsars and communists used censorship to control the freedom of expression. Successive governments tended to retain the right to withdraw publications thought to include 'dangerous orientation' (criticism of regimes). Government departments under the tsars used their own newspapers (*Ruskii*) to publish official news. There was some relaxation of control under Nicholas II and, as a result, newspapers aimed at the proletariat appeared, most notably the *Kopek*. The communists made great use of censorship. Under Stalin writers of all kinds were 'guided' to produce material to show '**socialist realism**' – accounts of the struggles of ordinary people to overcome oppression. Khrushchev eased censorship but the most popular newspapers were still those of an official variety, such as *Pravda* (paper of the Communist Party) and *Izvestiya* (paper of the government).

Religious freedom

Religious freedom under the tsars

Orthodox religion under the tsars emanated from the **Russian Orthodox Church**. Non-Orthodox religious groups, such as the Old Believers and Sectarian, Catholic, Protestant, Jewish and Muslim people, were tolerated. However, some leaders encouraged members of such groups to convert.

Religious freedom under the communists

After the revolution the Bolsheviks placed severe restrictions on the activities of the Russian Orthodox Church. They issued the 'Decree on the Separation of the Church from the State and the School from the Church', which involved the withdrawal of state subsidies and prevented religious groups from possessing property (including icons). This set the pattern of repression of religion in Russia until the end of the period.

Develop the detail

Below is a sample exam question and a paragraph written in answer to this question. The paragraph contains a limited amount of detail. Annotate the paragraph to add additional detail to the answer.

> To what extent did the Russian people have more freedom under the tsars than under communist rule in the period from 1855 to 1964?

When it came to the people being allowed to express their views through the media, tight restrictions were imposed by both the tsars and the communists. The tsars and communists used censorship to control freedom of expression. Successive governments tended to retain the right to withdraw publications. Government departments under the tsars used their own newspapers but there was some relaxation of control over the press under Nicholas II. The communists were heavily into censorship. Under Stalin, writers of all kinds were persuaded to write only certain kinds of material. Khrushchev eased censorship but the media still tended to present only the official view of events.

 Recommended reading

Below is a list of suggested further reading on this topic.

- Andrew Holland, *Access to History: Russia and its Rulers 1855–1964* (2016), pages 122–28
- Orlando Figes, *Revolutionary Russia, 1891–1991* (2014)
- Geoffrey Hosking, *Russia and the Russians: From Earliest Times to 2001* (2002)
- Robert Service, *A History of Modern Russia: From Nicholas II to Putin* (2003)

Exam focus

Below is a sample of a higher-level essay. Read the essay and the comments around it.

'The tsars did more than communist rulers to improve the living and working conditions of peasants in the period from 1855 to 1964.' How far do you agree?

In the period from 1855 to 1917 the tsars introduced major agricultural reforms but they were not wholly successful in improving the working and living conditions of rural people. There were a number of similarities between the agricultural policies pursued by the tsars and those pursued by communist leaders. Both the tsars and the communists were more concerned with industrialisation, and both saw the peasantry in a negative light. On the other hand, there were also clear differences. In particular, Stalin sought to eradicate the 'bourgeois' peasant class favoured by the tsars, and instead aimed to collectivise farms under centralised direction. Overall, the claim that the tsars did more than the communists to help peasants is slightly misleading; both regimes failed to prioritise peasant needs although Stalin's policies stand out as being quite harsh.

When it came to basic freedoms, the tsars certainly seem to have done more to help peasants. Alexander II freed serfs through the Emancipation Edict (1861), although their activities were still partially restricted by the *mir*. This freedom continued under Alexander III and Nicholas II, although the introduction of Land Captains (1889) resulted in close scrutiny of the actions of peasants appointed to *Zemstva* (councils). Under Nicholas II peasant freedom was generally respected and even furthered through Stolypin's 'wager on the strong'. Stolypin's policies resulted in the consolidation of land into smallholdings and greater peasant independence as producers. Initially, under Lenin, peasant freedoms were eroded – War Communism involved grain requisitioning and conscription of peasants into the Red Army to fight in the Civil War. There was some respite with Lenin's New Economic Policy, which once again encouraged peasants to produce food surpluses which could be sold at markets for profit. However, under Stalin collectivisation was established – peasants were forced onto collective farms which once again led to a loss of freedom to work as they wished. Stalin also purged rural society of wealthier peasants (kulaks), which further supports the notion that the communists dealt with the lower rural classes more brutally than the tsars.

With respect to land allocation, through the 1861 Emancipation Edict peasants received land to farm independently – but the obligation to pay redemption dues meant that land ownership was costly. In fact, in the long run many peasants struggled to pay back what they owed and were forced to sell their plots. Also, allocations were often relatively small and of poor quality. The introduction of the Peasant Land Bank (1883) by Alexander III helped to ease the burden of land purchase but the problem of land allocation remained. In contrast to the tsars, Lenin promised the peasants 'Peace, Bread and Land', but only kulaks seemed to benefit (through the New Economic Policy). Stalin's collectivisation meant that most land was the property of the state – this bore similarities to the pre-emancipation land ownership system and can therefore be viewed as a backward step for peasants. Khrushchev's Virgin Lands scheme also failed to address peasant land concerns. It was designed mainly to utilise land that had been previously left barren. Thus, the land issue was not resolved during the period – in this respect, neither the tsars nor the communists were successful in improving peasant conditions.

Any peasants that tried to voice concerns about their plight were dealt with severely by all Russian leaders. Both the tsars and the communists were more concerned with industrialisation and how the peasantry could best serve the needs of a growing urban population. Dissent by peasants was generally viewed as an obstacle to the need to provide workers with more food. Thus, rural revolts after the announcement of the 1861 Edict were put down by the military, resulting in the death of over 200 peasants, Land Captains were quick to deal with renewed protests in the 1890s, and the Black Earth revolts of 1906–07 were ended by the intervention of the army, directed by Stolypin. Lenin continued to repress

This is a long but clearly stated introduction that both outlines the line of argument to be taken and displays a good awareness of the need to compare and contrast the policies of different rulers.

The basic theme of freedoms is discussed here in detail. A very good understanding of the key concepts of continuity and change is evident.

Another key theme is analysed here and the candidate proves adept in looking at the similarities and differences between the policies on land adopted by Russian leaders. Very good synthesis and synoptic assessment of the whole period is displayed.

The candidate has sustained a synoptic approach and has been skilful in blending in judgements about the degree of brutality used by tsars and communists in dealing with peasant protesters.

Quick quizzes at **www.hoddereducation.co.uk/myrevisionnotes**

dissident peasants, particularly over grain requisitioning, using the Cheka. Such repression was continued by Stalin as shown by the enforcement of collectivisation. Those who opposed the policy were either arrested and executed or sent to Gulags. Under Khrushchev the harsh treatment of peasants was eased when they complained, but in general the tsars and the communists were equally brutal in dealing with peasant rebellion.

There was some change in basic peasant living conditions over the period. The standard house remained the *izba*, a single-room wooden hut heated by an oven which also acted as a sleeping platform. Animals were accommodated in the hut alongside families. Although the huts were cheap to construct, the living conditions experienced by peasants were cramped, cold and damp. Under Stalin there was some change in the way peasants were housed. 'Special' housing blocks were constructed on the periphery of the new collective farms. However, kulaks were often allocated the worst housing in barracks or forced into tented shelter in fields. Khrushchev ordered the construction of self-contained 'agro-towns' for peasants but these were built cheaply and quickly and were inadequate. Thus, by modern standards, peasant housing remained uniformly poor.

As peasants made up the vast majority of Russian society, they were always most likely to feel the brunt of the fairly frequent famines that hit Russia. Some of the food shortages were actually engendered by Russian leaders and the tsars or the communists seldom dealt effectively with famine. In 1891 adverse weather coupled with the panic selling of grain surpluses to counter the impact of a new consumer goods tax resulted in food shortages. Peasants sold the surpluses to pay for increases in the tax. Over 350,000 people died. Disruption to trade and transport during the First World War also led to food shortages. The crisis was made worse by Lenin sanctioning the signing of the Treaty of Brest-Litovsk whereby valuable grain-producing areas in the Ukraine were lost. In 1921 terrible winters, severe droughts and destruction of transport infrastructures due to the Civil War combined to create a famine in which up to 6 million people died. The problem was exacerbated by Lenin's slow response to the crisis and his reluctance to accept aid from the American Relief Agency. Once again leaders failed to alleviate the hardship experienced by peasants. The Great Famine of 1932–34 saw similar mortality levels to those of 1921, but suffering was made worse by the repression of the people by Stalin. For example, the death penalty was imposed on people for stealing grain. Thus, in terms of ensuring that peasants were adequately fed, both the tsars and the communists could be said to be equally negligent.

In conclusion, it is hard to sustain the argument that the tsars did more to improve the living and working conditions of rural people. Although the abolition of serfdom was a major turning point, rural people still lived a very harsh life, with insufficient access to good land, machinery or credit. Similarly, although the Bolsheviks initiated land reforms to help rural people, they were more concerned with industrialisation. Thus, the tsars did not treat peasants better than the communists. Some positive measures were undertaken to help peasants but in general, all Russian leaders seemed to treat peasants with contempt.

> This is a useful section on peasant housing conditions, although some of the comments could have been supported with a little more detail.

> The impact of famine on peasants is dealt with very effectively here. Once again, some comparisons are made and the theme is clearly linked to the question.

> This is a clear, balanced conclusion. The overall judgement made is congruent with the main body of the essay. Most importantly, there is no attempt to introduce new material to the answer.

This essay uses a good range of accurate and relevant evidence. A range of themes are considered and analysed. The use of synthesis is mostly sustained throughout and the candidate reaches a well-considered conclusion. The answer is also clearly structured and coherent.

Synthesis words

The key to a good Themes answer is to synthesise material. Go through the response and identify all the words that indicate that synthesis is being used (for example, 'linked to', 'compared with'). Then find places where synthesis could be developed further (ask yourself whether all the sections in the answer make links across the period).

3 The impact of war and revolution on the development of the Russian Empire and the USSR

The Crimean War, 1853–56

The Crimean War was fought between Russia and the **Ottoman** Turks, with the latter supported by Britain and France. The war culminated in the Siege of Sevastopol, during which Russian troops surrendered, and the signing of the Treaty of Paris (1856). The Treaty resulted in Russia ceding valuable territory in Bessarabia.

The effects of the Crimean War, 1853–56

The war affected the development of the government of the Russian Empire in the following ways:

- Alexander II associated lack of success in the war with the idea that compared to Britain and France, Russia's economic and social infrastructure was outdated. In particular, serfdom was geared towards an economy based on agricultural production, tightly controlled by the aristocratic classes. The emphasis on control by the nobility went hand in hand with the desire to preserve autocracy and the Romanov dynasty.
- However, the emancipation of the serfs in 1861 allowed for greater entrepreneurialism in agriculture (for example, by selling surpluses at markets without the permission of the *mir*), the movement of some rural labour to industry, modernisation of the military and social reforms without the nobility and tsar losing their authority.
- Modernisation of the military occurred as emancipation meant that peasants had less of an obligation to serve as conscripts in the army. Thus, the tsar was able to change how the army was recruited, trained and organised.
- Most importantly, though, emancipation forced changes to be made to the way localities were governed. As the nobility saw their land holdings reduced, along with the obligations that went with serfdom, they no longer had much of a political role to play at a local level. Emancipated peasants seemed isolated from the rest of society with no outlet to express their grievances. By default, the management of local affairs was left in the hands of local police constables appointed by the **Interior Ministry**. Alexander II bridged this gap by introducing the institution of the *Zemstva*.

The creation of the *Zemstva*

The *Zemstva* appeared to bring an element of democracy to Russian government, but their importance must not be overstated.

Strengths of the *Zemstva*	Limitations of the *Zemstva*
Members were elected by a mixture of landowners, urban dwellers and peasants based on a property qualification.	The councils tended to be dominated by the nobility and professional classes.
The *Zemstva* could feed regional issues back to central government and, to an extent, challenge the policies of the tsar.	The *Zemstva* were located only in areas considered to be part of Great Russia – they were not to be found in Poland, the Baltic region or the Caucasus.
	For various reasons, not all of the provinces eligible for representation were covered by *Zemstva* – by 1917 there were still 37 provinces without one.

The limitations of reforms

The war did not lead to any major change in ideology and the structure of central Russian government. Alexander II's main aim was to preserve autocracy. The emancipation edict and its spin-offs (especially the *Zemstva*) were reforms from 'above', designed to counter what might have been an attempt to reform from 'below'. The tsar was astute enough to realise that discontent over Russia's performance in the war may have led to rebellion.

Support or challenge?

Below is a sample exam question which asks how far you agree with a specific statement. Below this is a series of general statements which are relevant to the question. Using your own knowledge and the information from the opposite page and material from the rest of section 3, decide whether these statements support or challenge the statement in the question and tick the appropriate box.

'The Crimean War had a greater impact on the development of the government of the Russian Empire than any other conflict in the period from 1855 to 1964.' How far do you agree with this view?

	SUPPORT	CHALLENGE
The Treaty of Paris was enacted in March 1856, highlighting the weak position of Russia.		
The emancipation of the serfs did not happen immediately after the Crimean War.		
Alexander II introduced the *Zemstva* to link central government with the localities.		
Military reforms were introduced between 1862 and 1874.		
Education reforms also happened during the reign of Alexander II (see page 32).		
The effects of the Russo-Turkish War on social policy were negligible.		
The Russo-Japanese War was closely linked to the 1905 Revolution.		
The impact of the revolutions of 1917 on the Russian economy was far-reaching.		
The Second World War was closely linked to the Cold War, both of which were financially damaging to Russia.		

 Simple essay style

Below is a sample exam question. Use your own knowledge, information on the opposite page and information from other sections of the book to produce a plan for this question. Choose four general points and provide three pieces of specific information to support each general point.

Once you have planned your essay, write the introduction and conclusion for the essay. The introduction should list the points to be discussed in the essay. The conclusion should summarise the key points and justify which point was the most important.

How influential was the Crimean War on the development of Russian government in comparison to other conflicts in the period from 1855 to 1964?

The Russo-Japanese War and revolution, 1904–05

Russia's relationship with Japan before 1904

Prior to 1904, Russia and Japan had quarrelled for many years over Korea and **Manchuria**. Generally, Russia had looked to increase its influence in the Far East – of particular note was Russia's success in negotiating a 25-year lease of the strategically placed Port Arthur from the Chinese.

Russia increased its threat to Japan with the construction of the Chinese Eastern Railway and occupation of Manchuria, following a short military conflict with the Chinese. Russia actually agreed to withdraw its troops from Manchuria in 1903 but then reneged on the agreement. In February 1904 the Japanese retaliated by attacking Port Arthur – this was the spark for the Russo-Japanese War.

The course of the war

The war was a disaster for Russia. Russian forces were defeated at the Battle of Yalu, Port Arthur surrendered and the Russian naval fleet was trounced in the Tsushima Straits. The final straw was a humiliating defeat at the Battle of Mukden. The resultant Treaty of Portsmouth (August 1905) was humiliating for Russia. It was made to withdraw from Manchuria and Port Arthur and had to acknowledge Japanese sovereignty over Korea.

The effects of the Russo-Japanese War, 1904–05

The consequences of the war for the development of Russian government were as follows:
- The tsar and his government were blamed for losing the war to a country considered to be inferior in every sense. Discontent in Russia mounted in 1904 and 1905. Plehve, Minister of the Interior, was assassinated in July 1904.
- Restrictions had been imposed on *Zemstva* activity by Alexander III as a result of members voicing too many complaints about how the tsar ruled. They were lifted by Nicholas II in an attempt to gain support from the *Zemstva* but, once again, this led to more open criticism of the tsar and demands for reform.
- In October 1905 Nicholas II published the October Manifesto, which outlined his plan for the introduction of a more representative form of government in the form of the *Duma*. These measures were introduced largely to appease the increasing number of opponents to the regime.
- At first the *Duma* appeared to be a revolutionary measure, as it represented a move towards a constitutional monarchy. However, the Fundamental Laws of 1906 meant that the tsar would retain autocratic control.

The war and the events of 1905: a revolution?

Historians often cite the following events of 1905 as evidence of reaction and protest against Russia's involvement in the Russo-Japanese War. Some even claim that the events constitute a revolution, especially as they seemed to influence the tsar's decision to set up a *Duma*.
- 3 January: Strike at Putilov works
- 9 January: Bloody Sunday
- March: Defeat of Russian army at Mukden
- June: All-Russian Union of Peasants established
- September: Mutinies in the army
- 8 October: Strike by railway workers
- 13 October: St Petersburg Soviet established
- 17 October: Nicholas II published the October Manifesto.

You will need to research these events further before coming to your own conclusion about whether 1905 was truly a revolutionary year.

Developing an argument

Below are a sample exam question, a list of key points to be made in the essay and a paragraph from the essay. Read the question, the plan and the sample paragraph. Rewrite the paragraph in order to develop an argument. Your paragraph should answer the question directly, and set out the evidence that supports your argument. Crucially, it should develop an argument by setting out a general answer to the question and reasons that support this.

'The Russo-Japanese War was the most important turning point in the development of Russian government in the period from 1855 to 1964.' How far do you agree?

Key points:

- Russia's relationship with Japan before 1904
- The course of the war
- The effects of the Russo-Japanese War: social unrest (revolution?)
- The October Manifesto (1905) and the creation of the *Duma*
- The Fundamental Laws (1906).

> The Russo-Japanese War of 1904–05 was significant because Russia struggled to beat an enemy that should have been dealt with easily. Russian defeats in battle, such as at Mukden, were humiliating for the government and angered the Russian people, who could not understand how the Russian military had lost to an 'unimportant' Asian country. This anger spilled over into a mini revolution. The tsar responded by creating the *Duma*, which allowed the population to have more say in the way the country was to be run. However, Nicholas clamped down on its powers (using the Fundamental Laws of 1906) so this was not such a big change after all. As a result of the Russo-Japanese War, Nicholas II also instructed his ministers to speed up industrialisation and to improve the railway system. Without this, Russia would never have been able to compete in a major conflict with the other European powers. Even though this was mostly successful, Russia still struggled to cope with the First World War.

 Develop the detail

Below is a sample question and a paragraph written in answer to it. The paragraph contains a limited amount of detail. Annotate the paragraph to include additional detail to the answer.

'Out of all the wars that influenced the development of Russian government, the Russo-Japanese War (1904–05) was the most significant.' How far do you agree?

> The impact of the Russo-Japanese War on the development of Russian government was certainly significant. It was the first war that, via social protest against its outcome, led to the creation of the first national assembly that was democratically elected. In contrast, the Crimean War only resulted in local representative bodies being created (alongside a limited franchise) and the First World War led to chaos in the Russian political system with the abdication of the tsar, the downfall of the inept and short-lived Provisional Government and the coming of a Bolshevik government, which dismissed democracy. Later in the period, the Second World War and Cold War had very little impact on the ideology, structure and tools of government. However, the creation of the *Duma* was not as revolutionary as it first seemed – Nicholas passed laws to ensure that autocratic control of government was maintained. The First World War and connected revolutions of 1917 were far more significant.

The First World War, 1914–18

Russia's involvement in the First World War was partly a result of a failure to resolve the **Eastern Question** satisfactorily (as witnessed by the **Balkan Wars of 1912–13**) but also due to deterioration in relations with **Austria–Hungary**. The famous Russian mobilisation order, which got the Russian military ready for war, resulted from the declaration of war by Austria–Hungary on Serbia in July 1914. Russia then had an obligation to support fellow Slavs.

As with the Crimean War and Russo-Japanese War, the First World War went badly for Russia. Russian casualties for the whole war were about 8 million (including 1.7 million dead and 2.4 million captured). Nicholas II's incompetence as wartime leader was partly responsible for his abdication in February 1917. The war eventually ended for Russia in December 1917 when peace talks were concluded at Brest-Litovsk.

An interesting way of assessing the impact of the war on Russian government is to consider two schools of thought: the optimists and the pessimists.

The optimists	The pessimists
Optimist historians believe that an event such as the First World War was necessary if autocracy in Russia was going to disappear forever.	The pessimists think that the war was not a turning point, as the tsars had been struggling for decades to deal with demands for constitutional reform. The war did not suddenly result in a clamour for change. Furthermore, Nicholas is viewed as a very incompetent leader and it is seen as only a matter of time before he was deposed and the Romanov dynasty was ended.
Military failures during the war resulted in economic challenges which impacted greatly on the daily lives of Russians on the home front. Social unrest grew to levels never seen before in Russia.	
The scale and degree of co-ordination required of the military forces and industry were such that the authorities struggled to cope. A drastic change in government was inevitable if a state of anarchy was to be averted.	Worker opposition to the government that increased during the war had also gathered momentum well before the war began. Working-class consciousness had emerged over time with the aid of the legalisation of political parties, the growth of trade unions and the setting up of soviets.
The war resulted in huge errors of judgement by the tsar. He took personal control of the armed forces (a task he performed badly), left the capital (Petrograd) and handed over control of domestic political affairs to his German wife, Alexandra. Her background, along with her friendship with the mystic Rasputin, resulted in great resentment among the Russian people.	
The result was the formation of the Provisional Government. The optimists believe this was a positive development and that it was only the unnecessary continuation of Russia's involvement in the war that caused the downfall of the new regime.	Thus, the pessimist view emphasises the importance of the efforts of workers over time which led to the abdication of the tsar, rather than external events.

Below is a sample exam question which asks how far you agree with a specific statement. Below this is a series of general statements which are relevant to the question. Using your own knowledge and the information on the opposite page, decide whether these statements support or challenge the statement in the question and tick the appropriate box.

'Compared to other wars in the period from 1855 to 1964, the impact of the First World War on Russian government has been exaggerated.' How far do you agree with this statement?'

	SUPPORT	CHALLENGE
Constitutional change was beginning to occur before the First World War.		
There was much social unrest as a result of the war.		
Pessimist historians believe that Nicholas II was an incompetent leader.		
When Nicholas II abdicated, Russia still did not pull out of the war.		
The *Duma* had developed a progressive bloc before the war began.		
Large-scale industrialisation had already sparked greater class consciousness.		

! **Delete as applicable**　　ⓐ

Below is a sample exam question and a paragraph written in answer to this question. Read the paragraph and decide which of the possible options (in bold) is most appropriate. Delete the least appropriate options and complete the paragraph by justifying your selection.

'The First World War had a more important impact on Russian government than any other conflict in the period from 1855 to 1964.' How far do you agree with this view?

To a **great/fair/limited** extent, the First World War was the most important conflict for the **development/overthrow** of Russian government from 1855 to 1964. Without the war, Nicholas II would **probably not/still** have abdicated, and it is **fairly/highly** likely that the Bolsheviks would never have gained power. However, there was already a progressive bloc in the *Duma* for a **short time/long time** before the **end/beginning** of the war. Therefore, it is **possible/probable/almost certain** that significant **political/governmental/constitutional** change would have happened regardless.

_____

_____

The February Revolution, 1917

Russia's participation in the First World War caused social and economic conditions to deteriorate, which in turn intensified criticism of Tsar Nicholas II and his governance. Matters came to a head in late February 1917, when a series of strikes and protests led to workers being fired upon by troops. Subsequently, about half of the Petrograd Garrison decided to join the protesters, and a Petrograd Soviet was formed to rule alongside the Provisional Duma Committee. In the face of this opposition, Nicholas II had little choice but to abdicate, doing so on 2 March 1917. An official Provisional Government was formed to deal with the situation until a Constituent Assembly could be elected.

The October Revolution, 1917

Throughout the summer of 1917, members of the Soviet, including a growing number of Bolsheviks, became increasingly frustrated with the Provisional Government. Their main grievances concerned economic issues and the nature of Russia's continuing participation in the war. In October, the Bolsheviks, having gained a majority of the membership of the Soviet, seized power from the Provisional Government. Since the 1917 revolutions were of such fundamental importance to Russian history, it is unsurprising that the impact of the revolutions on Russian government is contentious.

The impact of the revolutions on the government of the Russian Empire

The revolutions resulted in the following:

- The autocratic rule of the tsars was replaced by a Provisional Government which ruled along classically liberal lines – it issued decrees on political amnesty and freedom of speech.
- However, when the Bolsheviks came to power, Lenin promised to introduce a dictatorship of the proletariat which would lead to stateless communism – a **communist utopia**. This was not achieved – in reality, Bolshevik rule led to a totalitarian regime comparable to the autocracy of the tsars.
- Members of the Provisional Government were arrested when the Bolsheviks came to power. The '**old guard**' were replaced by new political figures who opposed the bourgeois establishment.
- Since the October Revolution was in essence a 'Petrograd revolution', the Bolsheviks needed to gain support from other regions. They encouraged the formation of soviets in other Russian towns and cities but faced opposition from supporters of the old regime.
- The Second All-Russian Congress of Soviets (October 1917) had given the Bolsheviks a mandate to rule on the basis that government would be truly soviet-based. On 27 October Congress was informed that the Bolsheviks had seized power from the Provisional Government. Most of Congress was relatively happy about this.
- However, the right-wing SRs and Mensheviks walked out of the Congress in protest – they thought this signalled the start of a Bolshevik monopoly of power, rather than shared authority through a coalition.
- The Bolsheviks allowed elections to the Constituent Assembly, but came second to the SRs. Lenin shut the Assembly down after a single day, claiming that it was 'elected on the old register'. This caused some uproar from non-Bolsheviks.
- In January 1918, the Third All-Russian Congress of the Soviets proclaimed the establishment of the Russian Soviet Federalist Republic. A new political structure was put into place with Sovnarkom at its centre.
- However, although members of Sovnarkom were the product of a chain of elections, the system was dominated by the Bolshevik Party, and Russia soon resembled a **single-party state**.

! Spot the mistake a

Below is a sample exam question and a paragraph written in answer to this question. Why does this paragraph not get into a high level on the generic mark scheme? Once you have identified the problem, rewrite the paragraph so that it displays the qualities of a high-level answer. The mark scheme on page 7 will help you.

> 'The 1917 October Revolution was the event that had the most influence on the development of government in the period from 1855 to 1964.' How far do you agree?

> The revolution brought the Bolsheviks to power. This put an end to the autocratic rule of the tsars. The Bolsheviks wanted to replace autocratic rule with the dictatorship of the proletariat. This would lead to a stateless society, a communist utopia. Therefore, the revolution had a really important impact on the structure of Russian government, because tsarist autocracy was very different from stateless communism.

! Support or challenge? a

Below is a sample exam question which asks how far you agree with a specific statement. Below this is a series of general statements that are relevant to the question. Using your own knowledge and the information on the opposite page, decide whether these statements support or challenge the statement in the question and tick the appropriate box.

Note that the statements relate to only part of the topic on Russian government, but the actual exam questions require students to cover at least a 100-year period (see the Introduction, page 5).

> 'The February Revolution of 1917 was the most important turning point which led to political change in the period from 1855 to 1964.' How far do you agree with this statement?

	SUPPORT	CHALLENGE
There were significant tensions between the Provisional Government and the Petrograd Soviet.		
When Kerensky was made Prime Minister he reacted strongly against those involved in the July Days rising.		
The Bolsheviks were viewed as heroes in the aftermath of the Kornilov affair.		
Right-wing SRs and Mensheviks walked out of the Second All-Russian Congress of Soviets.		
The Bolsheviks encouraged other towns and cities to set up soviets.		
Lenin allowed elections to the Constituent Assembly.		
There was little opposition when Lenin abolished the Constituent Assembly.		

The Civil War, 1917–22

A number of different political and regional groups responded to the October Revolution by challenging the Bolsheviks. Some saw it as an opportunity to attack and destroy the Bolsheviks, while others were keen to gain independence from Russian central government. The resulting tensions led to the outbreak of a civil war. Although the Red Army was victorious, the Civil War lasted for five years, which showed the extent of and serious threat posed by opposition forces.

The course of the Civil War

The key events of the war were:

- November 1917: Kerensky's and General Krasnov's counter-offensive was brought to a halt.
- April 1918: Having defeated General Kornilov's Volunteer Army, Lenin proclaimed that the war was about to end. Foreign intervention occurred in this month, when British marines were sent to support the Whites.
- December 1918–end of 1920: White armies fought against the Reds. The Red Army, based mainly in Moscow, initially absorbed attacks from the Whites from all directions and then counter-attacked to score notable victories. Certain regions, such as the Ukraine, also demanded to be freed from central control as they believed they should be allowed to develop a separate national identity. By February there were signs that the resistance from the nationalists was receding.
- April 1921: Polish armed forces attacked Russia and reached as far as Kiev in the east. Russian forces counter-attacked and pushed the Poles back to Warsaw.
- August 1921: Another counter-attack in August, this time by Poland, resulted in the Red Army retreating.
- October 1921: The Russo-Polish conflict eventually came to a halt when the Treaty of Riga was signed.
- November 1921: Red forces drove out the last of the White troops from southern Russia.
- Throughout 1921: Groups of armed peasants formed to oppose the Bolsheviks. They were known as the Green armies. Their aim was to gain more freedoms from Bolshevik leaders.

The effects of the Civil War

The war affected Bolshevik domestic and foreign policies (more than other aspects of government) in a number of ways.

Foreign policy

- The strength of opposition forced Lenin to adopt a conciliatory foreign policy with other nations, although the Bolsheviks did not abandon the **Comintern** and the idea of 'world revolution'.
- Foreign intervention during the war had indicated to Lenin that he needed to try to reassure Western powers such as Britain, France and the USA that Russia did not represent a threat.
- Particularly influential on foreign policy was Russia's defeat by an inferior army in the Polish campaign, and foreign intervention on behalf of the Whites.

Domestic policy

- The Civil War was won through strong discipline, administration and management. This ethos influenced subsequent government, since many of those who served in the post-war government had also served in the Red Army.
- The introduction of War Communism included the nationalisation of large enterprises and a state monopoly of markets, as well as the partial militarisation of labour and the forced requisitioning of agricultural goods.
- War Communism caused significant unrest and, after the Civil War, Lenin replaced it with the NEP, denationalising small-scale businesses and giving peasants greater freedom to sell surplus products.
- The short-term impact of the NEP was extremely beneficial, but by the mid-1920s critics within the party became more vociferous.
- Partly to quell any internal unrest power became more centralised than before, revolving around the Politburo and the Orgburo. These party sub-committees became the key organs of government.

ⓘ Delete as applicable **a**

Below is a sample exam question and a paragraph written in answer to this question. Read the paragraph and decide which of the possible options (in bold) is most appropriate. Delete the least appropriate options and complete the paragraph by justifying your selection.

'In comparison with other conflicts in the period from 1855 to 1964, the Civil War had a very limited impact on the foreign policy of Russian government.' How far do you agree with this statement?

> The humiliation caused by defeat in the Polish campaign influenced Bolshevik foreign policy to a **limited/ fair/great** extent. As a result of foreign opposition, Russian relations with other countries became **much/a little** more peaceful, since Lenin was put on the defensive and had to show other countries that Russia was not expansionist. The idea of world revolution was not abandoned, but placed **somewhat/completely** on the backburner.
>
> _____
>
> _____

ⓘ Spider diagram

Use the information on the opposite page to add detail to the spider diagram below, to enable you to assess the impact of the Civil War on Russian government.

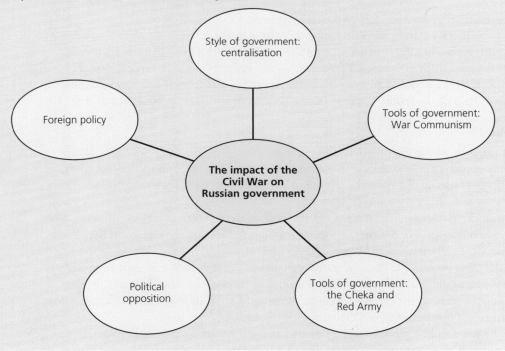

REVISED

The impact of the war on the Russian government

Although Germany and Russia signed a Nazi-Soviet Pact in 1939, peace between the two countries was never likely to be maintained. The Russian leadership believed the pact would give the country time to prepare for a possible attack by either Japan or Germany. Between 1939 and 1941 Russia remained neutral, but in June 1941 Nazi Germany implemented Operation Barbarossa and began an invasion of the USSR. In the ensuing conflict over 27 million Russians were killed, two-thirds of whom were civilians. Although the war had significant social and economic effects, the political impact was more limited.

Ideology

Since the USSR's government was already much centralised and authoritarian it would be difficult to argue that it became even more totalitarian as a result of the war, especially as the circumstances of the conflict forced other governments to adopt similar authoritarian measures.

Structure

The structure of government remained relatively stable.
- Stalin assumed the role of Supreme Commander of the Military and became Chairman of the State Defence Committee, which gave him absolute control of the military and those working in factories to supply the armed forces.
- However, Stalin still listened to his advisers, especially key members of the Politburo (**Molotov**, **Voroshilov**, **Kaganovich**, **Mikoyan**, **Andreyev** and Khrushchev), and relied on their judgement – all of these men retained their positions after the war.

Tools

The use of repression remained as a key tool of government.
- The NKVD was active during the war, and this continued after 1945.
- However, whereas during the conflict minority groups suspected of collaborating with the Nazis were targeted, such as Balkans, Chechens, Karachays and Crimean Tartars, after the conflict the NKVD reverted to purging the party and other dissidents. The cult of personality was also strengthened as a result of Stalin's 'heroic' efforts in pushing the Nazis out of Russia.

Foreign policy

The war had a significant impact on Soviet foreign relations.
- The wartime conferences held at Tehran (November–December 1943) and Yalta (February 1945) confirmed Russian claims to the territorial frontiers established under the Nazi-Soviet Pact (1939).
- After the war, the victorious Western powers allowed Stalin to exert a sphere of influence over much of Eastern Europe. For Stalin, this was critical in helping maintain a physical barrier between the West and the western Russian borderland.
- Others in the West viewed the Russian territorial gains as the start of Soviet expansionism with the long-term intention of promoting communism throughout the whole of Europe.
- Churchill later referred to the 'barrier' between West and East as an Iron Curtain; some claim that the first use of this term marked the start of the Cold War.
- The issue of what should happen to Germany after the war ended up causing the Soviet leadership difficulties. Germany as a whole, but also Berlin in particular, was divided into zones which were to be occupied by the allies until a stable German government could be set up. Russia had jurisdiction over the eastern zones but there was mutual suspicion and tensions between the occupying forces right from the start.
- The **Berlin Blockade** of 1948 and the erection of the **Berlin Wall** worsened relations between Russia and the West. The result of this was that the key problem of unifying Germany was never resolved until communism started to collapse throughout Europe over 40 years later.

Develop the detail

Below is a sample exam question and a paragraph written in answer to it. The paragraph contains a limited amount of detail. Annotate the paragraph to add additional detail to the answer.

> To what extent did the Second World War alter the nature of Russian government more than any other conflict in the period from 1855 to 1964?

> The Second World War influenced the structure of government to a limited extent. This was mainly because Stalin was already very powerful before the war. When Nazi Germany invaded Russia, Stalin assumed the role of war leader. Nicholas II had also been a war leader, but there were differences between how he acted during the First World War and how Stalin acted during the Second World War.

Turning assertion into argument

Below are a sample exam question and a series of assertions. Read the exam question and then add a justification to each of the assertions to turn it into an argument.

> 'The Second World War influenced Russian government more than any other conflict in the period from 1855 to 1964.' How far do you agree?

> The Second World War, compared to other military conflicts that Russia was involved in, had little impact on the structure of government because
>
> _____
>
> _____

> The impact of the Second World War on the NKVD was significant in that
>
> _____
>
> _____

> The Second World War, more than other military conflicts, had a significant bearing on Soviet foreign policy as a tool of government because
>
> _____
>
> _____

The Cold War, 1947–91

The Cold War involved simmering tension between the USSR and the West which stopped short of actual physical combat. The beginning and course of the Cold War before 1964 was marked by the following series of events.

- March 1947: US President Truman responded to the possibility of communist governments being established in Greece and Italy by issuing the **Truman Doctrine**.
- June 1947: The **Marshall Plan** for the economic recovery of Europe was presented by the USA. It was rejected by the Soviet Foreign Minister, Molotov, as the Russians believed it was a scam to spread capitalism.
- September 1947: The USSR set up **Cominform** – this was intended to counter the Marshall Plan but was disbanded in 1956.
- April 1949: The North Atlantic Treaty Organisation (NATO) was founded. Members of this group agreed to support each other if they were attacked by an aggressor. Those who belonged to it were anti-communist and it was obvious that NATO was designed to combat the perceived threat from the Soviet Union.
- June 1948–May 1949: The Berlin Blockade occurred.
- May 1955: The Warsaw Pact was formed. This involved the signing of a peace and security treaty by the Soviet Union, Albania, Bulgaria, Hungary, the GDR (East Germany), Poland, Romania and Czechoslovakia.
- October 1956: The Hungarian Revolution began. This was a popular uprising in Hungary, following a speech by Soviet leader Nikita Khrushchev in which he attacked the period of Stalin's rule. On 4 November the Soviet Union invaded Hungary to prevent the 'revolution' getting out of hand.
- August 1961: Construction of the Berlin Wall began.
- May 1962: A US U2 spy plane was shot down while flying over Russia. Khrushchev demanded an apology from US President Eisenhower.

The effects of the Cold War on Russian government

The war led to significant changes to Russian political ideology and domestic and foreign policies.

The impact on ideology

When Khrushchev came to power, he enacted a policy of de-Stalinisation in an attempt to present a more favourable picture of Russia to the West.

The impact on domestic policy

The Cold War prompted an arms race which required high levels of investment in heavy industry. This prevented more investment in consumer products and caused unrest, such as the Novocherkassk worker protests, 1962. This was dealt with ruthlessly.

The impact on foreign policy

A number of situations, such as the Cuban Missile Crisis, nearly caused a war between the USSR and the USA. These incidents demonstrated that the Soviets were willing both to confront the Western countries and also to compromise.

The Cuban Missile Crisis, which ran from September 1962–January 1963, developed as follows:
- Summer 1962: Nikita Khrushchev secretly decided to install ballistic missiles in Cuba.
- October 1962: When US reconnaissance air-force flights revealed the construction of missile launch sites, US President Kennedy denounced Soviet actions.
- October 1962: The USA imposed a naval blockade on Cuba.
- 24 October 1962: Russian ships carrying missiles to Cuba turned back to Russia.
- 28 October 1962: Khrushchev agreed to dismantle the missile sites. The crisis ended as suddenly as it had begun.
- 20 November 1962: The USA ended its blockade of Cuba and promised not to go ahead with a planned invasion of the island.

Eliminate irrelevance a

Below is a sample exam question and a paragraph written in answer to this question. Read the paragraph and identify parts of the paragraph that are not directly relevant to the question. Draw a line through the information that is irrelevant and justify your deletions in the margin.

> To what extent did the Cold War affect the way Russia was governed in comparison to other conflicts in the period from 1855 to 1964?

> The Cold War was not a real war. The USSR and the West were enemies but did not actually fight each other. One of the most important events was the Cuban Missile Crisis. This involved the USSR trying to use Cuba as a place where missiles could be based. The USA opposed this and there was a big struggle. In some ways this affected the way Russia was governed. On the one hand, money had to be spent on military hardware to frighten the Americans. The Russian people did not always support this, because it meant other goods became more expensive. On the other hand, the Soviet government could use the confrontation to gain patriotic support for its actions.

Spectrum of importance

Below are a sample exam question and a list of general points which could be used to answer part of the question (that is, the part that would need discussion of how far the administration and structure of Russian government changed). Use your own knowledge and the information on the opposite page to reach a judgement about the importance of these general points to the question posed.

Write numbers on the spectrum below to indicate their relative importance. Having done this, write a brief justification of your placement, explaining why some of these factors are more important than others. The resulting diagram could form the basis of an essay plan.

> 'The Cold War was the least influential conflict which affected the way Russia was governed from 1855 to 1964.' How far do you agree with this statement?

1 The Crimean War

2 The October Manifesto

3 The 1917 Revolution

4 Operation Barbarossa

5 De-Stalinisation

6 The Cuban Missile Crisis.

Least important ←——————————————————————————————→ Most important

Exam focus

Below is a sample of a high-level essay. Read the essay and the comments around it.

'Out of all the wars that influenced the development of Russian government from 1855 to 1964, the Civil War (1917–22) was the most significant.' How far do you agree?

The Civil War influenced Russian government in a number of significant ways, such as encouraging a strict, militaristic way of governing, increasing centralisation and the nationalisation of industry through an economic policy called 'War Communism' and also affecting diplomatic relations with other nations. However, it was far less influential than conflicts which preceded it, out of which it grew. In particular, the First World War and the 1917 Revolution formed a far more important turning point, ending the autocracy of the tsars and paving the way for a single-party communist state.

> This is a clear introduction that gives an indication of how the candidate intends to make an overall judgement about the impact of the Civil War.

Bolshevik success during the war was partially due to the discipline of the Red Army, and also the strict administration put in place by Trotsky. This ethos of disciplined efficiency affected the nature of government after the war and influenced the way in which new bodies such as the Orgburo and Politburo worked. Indeed, a number of those who served in the Red Army were also active in government after the war. Moreover, power became even more centralised during and after the war, providing a template for subsequent government.

> The candidate has adopted the right approach by starting the essay with discussion of the importance of the named factor in the question. There is no comparison made with other wars. This is not vital here as long as synthesis is shown later in the essay.

A further major impact was the introduction of War Communism – it involved the nationalisation of large enterprises, a state monopoly of markets, the partial militarisation of labour and the requisitioning of agricultural goods. Although this policy was short-lived and replaced by the New Economic Policy (NEP) after the war, it caused significant unrest, as Lenin ordered the Cheka to enforce War Communism with considerable brutality. Secondly, it could be viewed as a continuation of the tsarist ideology of maintaining autocracy through policies controlled from the centre. Thirdly, the policy of War Communism encouraged mistrust of Russian leaders among the other great powers, who feared the spread of Bolshevism. The opposition of the international community forced Lenin to adopt a more conciliatory approach to diplomacy with foreign countries. In turn, this meant that the idea of 'world revolution' was less prominent although not entirely forgotten.

> There are well-explained observations here about the impact of the Civil War, with an emphasis on how government was affected.

Certainly, without the Bolshevik victory in the Civil War, the impact of the Revolution would have been very different. The autocratic rule of the tsars may have been reintroduced, or the structure of government may have been altered in some other way. On the other hand, without the First World War and the 1917 Revolution, it is possible that tsarist autocracy would have survived, and that there would never have been any possibility of imposing a communist form of government on Russia. Thus, since the Civil War was the result of the First World War and the Russian Revolution, these conflicts were arguably more influential. In particular, the First World War provided an opportunity for revolution. Military failure, such as the early defeats suffered at Tannenberg and the Masurian Lakes, sparked criticism of the existing political system. This was exacerbated by the perceived failings of Nicholas II as the commander-in-chief. His inadequate leadership, along with incidents such as the 'shells crisis' and the failure of the Brusilov offensive, dented the morale of the Russian people and their support for tsarism.

> Some effective links are made here between different wars. Synthesis is used as the basis of an argument about how the Civil War was less significant than the First World War and the revolutions of 1917. Also, the importance of the role of Nicholas II is highlighted.

However, although a number of historians have claimed that without the First World War tsarist rule (or a modified form) would likely have remained, a fair case can be proposed that the foundations for social revolution lay before the war, and therefore it was inevitable that political change would occur. Industrialisation and deteriorating living and working conditions, for example, had already sparked considerable social unrest. Secondly, it is questionable whether the revolution was really as revolutionary as it first appeared. Lenin and Stalin both ruled as dictators, a form of rule comparable to the autocratic style of government which characterised tsarist rule.

The more limited conflicts which occurred in the half-century before the First World War were less influential, although they did expose Russian weakness and therefore contributed to criticism of the existing forms of government. In particular, a loss of prestige was made apparent in the unfavourable terms which followed the Crimean War (1853–56), Russo-Turkish War (1877–78) and Russo-Japanese War (1904–05). For example, under the Treaty of Paris (1856), Russia lost Bessarabia to Moldavia and was allowed only restricted access to the Black Sea. Even after the Russo-Turkish War, which was relatively successful, Russia was forced to make concessions to Austria–Hungary at the Congress of Berlin (1878). These conflicts were also responsible for a number of reforms. The Crimean War was probably the catalyst for the emancipation of the serfs (1861) and the introduction of *Zemstva* (1864), regional councils which changed the nature of local government. Further political reform occurred at the end of the Russo-Japanese War, with the introduction of the *Duma* (1905), a more representative council. However, the Fundamental Laws of 1906 re-emphasised the all-encompassing powers of the tsar, and therefore the earlier reforms which introduced the *Zemstva* and *Dumas* seem more cosmetic than containing anything of substance.

In comparison to the conflicts up to and including the Civil War, those which occurred afterwards were less influential. Both the Second World War and the Cold War affected the nature of government to a far lesser extent. From 1941 until 1945 Stalin continued to exert complete control, assisted by the Politburo, the make-up of which remained largely the same. An important effect of the Second World War was the territorial gains made by the USSR and the increasing influence that Russia exerted over Eastern Europe. This caused political tensions as nationalists tended to resent Russian dominance. Similarly, the influence of the Cold War on government was subtle rather than pronounced. The need to compete with the United States forced Russian politicians to favour heavy industrialisation, which in turn meant that consumer products tended to be neglected. This sparked social unrest and contributed to the unravelling of the communist system.

All in all, however, it is difficult to see the Civil War, or the wars that came afterwards, as more influential than those which brought about Bolshevik rule. In particular, the First World War produced distinct circumstances in which a revolution could occur and a new ruling elite become entrenched. Thereafter, the persistence and shape of the new regime were contested, but not fundamentally altered.

A general point is made here about the importance of analysing the impact of the wars by placing them in the context of longer-term social and economic change. This is a useful point, although it could have been supported with more detailed material.

This contains a sustained piece of analysis and argument about the limited impact of wars before 1905. There is excellent synthesis here and a very good example of synoptic writing.

Another very good example of a comparative approach. The candidate shows a good understanding of the key concepts of change and continuity and has maintained strict relevance to the question.

The conclusion is very sound. It is straightforward and makes a clear judgement about the relative importance of the impact of the Civil War on Russian government.

This essay displays many of the qualities of answers that achieve the highest levels. There is analysis, some very good synthesis and a sustained argument about the relative importance of the Civil War to Russian government. Some of the judgements made are uneven and the discussion sometimes drifts from how Russian government was affected by war. However, the overall quality of this answer is good enough for it to be awarded a high-level mark.

4 Russia: Empire, nationalities and satellite states

Nationalities: context and definitions

Background

The composition and extent of the Russian Empire changed over time. There were occasions when a policy of expansionism and Russification resulted in Russian influence extending to the Polish border with Germany and, in the opposite direction, to the Far East. However, the Empire also shrank at times, mainly as a result of wars and revolution. Changes in central government often led to a rise in nationalist movements in parts of the Empire. Russian leaders, whether tsars or communists, dealt with nationalist uprisings either with force or by making concessions.

In the middle part of the nineteenth century the Russian empire consisted of:
- Great Russia
- the 'national minorities' (that is, those who did not originate from the Russian peoples).

Great Russia

Great Russians were people who lived in the territory which formed the Old Russian Principality. The centre of the region was Moscow – generally, the area was more industrial than the rest of Russia, with a higher density of population.

National minorities

The main national minority groups were from:
- Poland
- Finland
- the Caucasus and Central Asia
- the Baltic Provinces (Estonia, Latvia and Lithuania).

Russian Jewish people stand out as a unique national minority in that their geographical location was one that was artificially created and crossed the boundaries of other groups. The significance of national minorities is highlighted in the results of the first Russian census of 1897 – for example, it was revealed that minorities made up about 55 per cent of the Empire's population in the Ukraine.

Not all national minorities opposed the ruling elites during the tsarist and communist periods. In general:
- The Finns, Baltic Germans and Christian Armenians remained fairly loyal.
- The Poles, Ukrainians and Tartars were a constant thorn in the side of Russian rulers.

From the point of view of the tsars and communists, this did not seem to matter, as they were all treated roughly the same. All leaders, to a greater or lesser extent, aimed to Russify minorities in what, with hindsight, proved to be a naïve and unrealistic attempt to create internal stability.

The main objective of the 'unco-operative' national minorities was, of course, to break away from central Russian rule and to gain independence. The experience of each national minority group in attempting to achieve autonomy varied according to time and place. For example, in Poland in 1864, the Milyutin Plan meant that:
- Hundreds of members of the Polish nobility were exiled to Siberia – their estates were transferred to incoming Russian officials who were to take over the duties of the nobles.
- Polish peasants were emancipated and gained even more favourable terms than their Russian counterparts had done in 1861. They gained freehold rights to allotted lands and paid for this through a reformed taxation system. The latter resulted in all landowners paying tax (not just peasants) to compensate those who had property redistributed.
- Rural district councils were set up (similar to the *Zemstva*) and were to contain members from all sections of Polish society.

However, after the Russo-Polish War of 1920 this situation was reversed and Poland entered into a stable period of independent rule. In comparison, for Russian Jewish people the question of independence never arose as they never had a homeland within the Russian Empire. For this group, their main aim was to gain and maintain freedom and justice.

Simple essay style

Below is a sample exam question. Use your own knowledge and the information on the opposite page to produce a plan for this question. Choose four general points and provide three pieces of specific information to support each general point.

Once you have planned your essay, write the introduction and conclusion for the essay. The introduction should list the points to be discussed in the essay. The conclusion should summarise the key points and justify which point was the most important.

To what extent did the composition and extent of the Russian Empire change from 1855 to 1964?

Support or challenge?

Below is a sample exam question which asks how far you agree with a specific statement. Below this is a series of general statements which are relevant to the question. Using your own knowledge and the information on the opposite page, decide whether these statements support or challenge the statement in the question.

To what extent did Russian leaders treat national minorities in the same way in the period from 1855 to 1964?

	SUPPORT	CHALLENGE
The Milyutin Plan (1864) provided improved living and working conditions for Poles.		
Most Russian leaders, to a greater or lesser extent, adopted Russification.		
Russian Jewish people were never given independence.		
Poles, Ukrainians and Tartars opposed interference from rulers and had to be tightly controlled.		
Some Russian leaders were lenient towards the Finns, Baltic Germans and Armenians due to the loyalty they displayed.		

Establish criteria

Below is a sample exam question which requires you to make a judgement. The key term in the question has been underlined. Defining the meaning of the key term can help you establish criteria that you can use to make a judgement. Read the question, define the key term and then set out two or three criteria based on the key term, which you can use to reach and justify a judgement.

'Of all the national minority groups in Russia it was the Ukrainians that posed the greatest threat to the stability of central government in the period from 1855 to 1964.' How far do you agree?

Definition:

_____

_____

Criteria to judge whether the Ukrainians, of all the national minority groups, posed the greatest threat to the stability of central government in Russia from 1855 to 1964:

_____

_____

Russo-Polish relations, 1863–1964

Background

By the time that Alexander II took over as tsar, Poland was firmly under Russian control. Nevertheless, located on the western edge, Poland had never 'obviously' been part of the Russian Empire and the Poles had a long history of attempting to break away from tsarist rule. Such an attitude prevailed, and between 1918 and 1939 Poland gained independence. But by the end of the period, and due mainly to the impact of the Second World War, the Poles returned to being under the guidance and influence of a Russian government.

Continuity in Russo-Polish relations, 1863–1964

The events in the table below indicate how Russo-Polish relations ebbed and flowed.

Event	Explanation of continuity
The Polish Revolt, 1863	Alexander II's reforms gave hope to Polish nationalists that they would gain full independence. The Polish government, led by Wielopolski, rejected demands for full independence, which led to rebellion. The Milyutin Plan ended the revolt and left Poland under the firm control of Russia.
The Russo-Polish War, 1920	On 16 October 1920 an armistice between Poland and Russia was signed. Polish independence was confirmed and it was agreed that Western Ukraine and Western Belorussia should come under Polish authority. The freedom and territory gained in 1920 was to remain in place until immediately following the Second World War.

Change in Russo-Polish relations, 1863–1964

Event	Explanation of change
The impact of the First World War on Russo-Polish relations	Russia was forced to give up jurisdiction over Warsaw and Vilna, the centres of the Vistula region. Poland was free from Russian rule although official independence was not granted until 1918 with the signing of the Treaty of Brest-Litovsk (see page 66).
The lead-up to the Second World War and Russo-Polish relations	By the end of the inter-war period it was clear that Poland's fate was to be determined by Nazi policies and the way in which Russia, in particular, responded to them. The Nazi-Soviet pact of August 1939, coupled with the appeasement policy of Britain and France, gave Germany a 'green light' to invade Poland.
The impact of the Second World War on Russo-Polish relations	The Polish government escaped to London. Their demands for an investigation into the Katyn massacre led to Russia refusing to maintain diplomatic relations. The Russian offensive against Germany in 1944 and the establishment of the National Liberation Committee in Lublin suggested that post-war Poland might be governed by Russian sympathisers.
The wartime conferences: Yalta, Potsdam and the Polish Question	The conferences had the following consequences for Poland: February 1945, Yalta: Stalin demanded that a new Russo-Polish frontier be established along the so-called Curzon Line and that the whole of Poland be governed by a Soviet-backed Lublin-style regime. Roosevelt and Churchill acquiesced. July 1945, Potsdam: This conference dealt with the issue of Poland's western border. Stalin persuaded Truman (Roosevelt died on 12 April 1945) and Churchill to accept a western demarcation at the 'Oder-Niesse Line', which was well inside ethnic Germany. Soviet-style government was created across the newly reconstituted Poland. In February 1947 a provisional constitution was instigated which set up a Council of State. The Council had almost total legislative and executive power and was dominated by the Stalinist-influenced Polish Workers' Party (PPR). In 1952, with the imposition of a Soviet-style constitution, Poland was officially renamed the People's Republic of Poland.
Khrushchev and Poland	Revelation of the contents of Khrushchev's 'Secret Speech' provoked a demand from Polish intellectuals for Stalinist politicians in Poland to stand down. Such requests were supported by workers through strike action. Khrushchev largely agreed to their demands – in October 1956 **Wladyslaw Gomulka** was released from prison to take over the leadership of Poland. What followed was an easing of control over the Polish people. Generally, until Khrushchev's removal from power in 1964, the Polish experienced elements of relief from the highly oppressive period of Stalinist rule.

(ᵢ) Identify the concept   **a**

Below are five sample exam questions based on some of the following concepts:

- **Cause** – questions concern the reasons for something, or why something happened
- **Consequence** – questions concern the impact of an event, an action or a policy
- **Change/continuity** – questions ask you to investigate the extent to which things changed or stayed the same
- **Similarity/difference** – questions ask you to investigate the extent to which two events, actions or policies were similar
- **Significance** – questions concern the importance of an event, an action or a policy.

Read each of the questions and work out which of the concepts they are based on.

> 'Opposition to Russian influence had little impact on the Russification of Poland from 1855 to 1964.' How far do you agree?

> To what extent did Russia's policy towards Poland change from 1855 to 1964?

> 'Wars were the main influence on Russo-Polish relations from 1855 to 1964.' How far do you agree?

> 'Rebellion was the most important consequence of Russian interference in Polish affairs from 1855 to 1964.' How far do you agree?

> 'There was more change than continuity in the way Russia dealt with Poland from 1855 to 1964.' How far do you agree?

(ᵢ) Identify key terms

Below is a sample question which includes a key word or term. Key terms are important because their meaning can be helpful in structuring your answer, developing an argument, and establishing criteria that will help form the basis of a judgement.

> 'Russo-Polish relations were affected mainly by the change from tsarism to communism in the period from 1855 to 1964.' How far do you agree?

- First, identify the key word or term. This will be a word or phrase that is important to the meaning of the question. Underline the word or phrase.
- Secondly, define the key phrase. Your definition should set out the key features of the phrase or word that you are defining.
- Third, make an essay plan that reflects your definition.
- Finally, write a sentence answering the question that refers back to the definition.

Now repeat the task, with the question below and consider how the change in key terms affects the structure, argument and final judgement of your essay.

> 'Russo-Polish relations were completely transformed by the change from tsarism to communism in the period from 1855 to 1964.' How far do you agree?

Russification

Russification was the process whereby non-Russian regions were drawn more securely into the framework of the Russian state. This involved administrative integration and the transmission of Russian language, religion and culture to national minorities. Such 'social Russification' was linked to economic integration that came about as a result of developments in telecommunications and transport. Russification started with the Polish Revolt of 1863 (see page 62) and was continued by Lenin, Stalin and Khrushchev, mainly through constitutional changes and repression.

Finland

A liberal stance on Finland was taken before 1894 – a separate parliament (*Diet*) and constitution for Finns existed by 1865. Under Nicholas II, Finland was 'encouraged' to join the Russian Empire but this caused opposition; in 1905 Finland was given full autonomy (although the agreement was quickly reneged on by Stolypin). It was the Treaty of Brest-Litovsk (see page 66) that enabled Finland to achieve lasting independence. Later, the Winter War (November 1939–March 1940) was an unsuccessful Russian attempt to regain influence over Finland; with the signing of the **Treaty of Friendship, Co-operation and Mutual Assistance** (1948), Finland was able to maintain a status of neutrality.

The Baltic provinces

The Baltic provinces consisted of Estonia, Latvia and Lithuania. At the start of the period, these provinces were strongly influenced by 'old' German rulers. German influence waned by the end of the nineteenth century. The coincidental rise in nationalism was never strong enough for independence to be achieved, and with the 1936 Constitution it was relatively easy for these states to be incorporated in the new federal system of Russian government. The Baltic provinces suffered during the later parts of the Second World War; mass deportations due to accusations of collaboration with the Nazis were instigated. After the war, the region became more stable with few incidents of rebellion.

The Ukrainians

The Ukrainians suffered similar treatment to the Poles under the tsars. However, the Treaty of Brest-Litovsk granted the Ukraine full independence. This was short-lived, as they were unable to oppose the Red Army during the Civil War. The Ukraine was a very important grain-producing area and Stalin's collectivisation programme was implemented there, but with opposition, to take advantage of its productive capacity. In theory, the position of the Ukraine improved under the 1936 Constitution (see page 14), but during and after the Second World War many Ukrainians were accused of being German collaborators. Those found guilty were either executed or transported to the far north.

The Caucasians

Those living in the Caucasus region of Russia were divided along religious lines (Christian and Muslim people). These divisions, coupled with the high level of illiteracy in the region, made Russification relatively easy. Nevertheless, populist movements arose to fight against repression. Of particular note were the Dashnaks and the Georgian Mensheviks, who proved to be very antagonistic towards Nicholas II. Georgia gained independence in 1920 but was 'retaken' by the Red Army in 1921. Stalin, in his role as Commissar for National Minorities, ruthlessly dealt with Georgian dissidents, although later he made a concession in the 1936 Constitution by providing Georgia with full republican status.

Jewish people

Jewish people did not have a homeland in the Russian Empire. Before the time of Alexander II, an artificial **Pale of Settlement** had been established. Alexander II allowed members of the Pale to migrate to other regions, but his son (Alexander III) clamped down on this – generally, the period from 1881 up to the First World War was one of repression of Russian Jewish people. The communists were just as suspicious towards Jewish people. More 'special' settlements were established in the 1930s but the Second World War saw bans being imposed on aspects of Jewish culture. This came from a perceived threat of Jewish people as subversives. Persecution continued after the war – Khrushchev suppressed a number of prominent Jewish technical specialists for anti-communist activity.

Support your judgement

Below are a sample exam question and two basic judgements. Read the exam question and the two judgements. Support the judgement that you agree with more strongly by adding a reason that justifies the judgement.

'From 1855 to 1964 the Russification process was successfully implemented.' How far do you agree?

Overall, Russian leaders had limited success in implementing the Russification process in the period from 1855 to 1964.

_____

_____

Generally, Russian leaders had great success in implementing the Russification process in the period from 1855 to 1964.

_____

_____

Tip: Whichever option you choose, you will have to weigh up both sides of the argument. You could use phrases such as 'whereas' or words like 'although' in order to help the process of evaluation.

Establish criteria

Below is a sample exam question which requires you to make a judgement. The key term in the question has been underlined. Defining the meaning of the key term can help you establish criteria that you can use to make a judgement.

Read the question, define the key term and then set out two or three criteria based on the key term, which you can use to reach and justify a judgement.

'The policy of Russification proved to be of great benefit to Russian leaders in the period from 1855 to 1964.' How far do you agree?

Definition:

_____

_____

Criteria to judge the extent to which the policy of Russification proved to be of great benefit to Russian leaders in the period from 1855 to 1964:

_____

_____

_____

_____

The impact of the First World War and the Treaty of Brest-Litovsk

Once the Bolsheviks had dealt with the issue of the Constituent Assembly they moved on to address how to withdraw from the First World War (see page 67). Lenin had promised to bring peace to the Russian people ('Peace, Bread and Land'), but doing so without it appearing that Russia was surrendering was a tricky business. Eventually, in March 1918, the Treaty of Brest-Litovsk was signed with Germany.

The origins of the Treaty

- On 23 October 1917 the Bolshevik and Soviet government issued a Decree on Peace which asked 'All the Belligerent Nations' to start peace talks based on 'no annexations or indemnities'.
- A group of Russian negotiators was sent, on 16 November, to Brest-Litovsk (a town in Belorussia) to meet a German delegation to discuss the possibility of an armistice – but the talks stalled.
- The German leadership soon became tired of the slowness of the Bolsheviks in attempting to broker a deal. On 9 February a separate treaty with the Ukrainians was signed. Germany offered protection over a period of time, after which the Ukraine would be guaranteed full independence.
- On 18 February 1918 the German leadership responded further to Russian dalliance by ordering a force of 700,000 troops to push deep into Russian territory. It took them just five days to advance over 150 miles towards Petrograd. This encouraged Germany, on 23 February, to demand even more stringent conditions for peace.
- The Central Committee called another meeting to discuss the renewed demands. Lenin wanted the terms to be accepted, Trotsky argued for no response to be given, while Bukharin continued to demand the war be carried on in the name of **revolutionary defencism**.
- Lenin got his way and on 3 March the Treaty was signed. Bukharin and the Left SRs resigned from the Soviet government.

The stipulations of the Treaty

The price of peace for Russia was high. Germany insisted on harsh territorial demands; much land was ceded by Russia which contained valuable resources.

Russia lost the following:
- Poland
- Estonia
- Latvia
- Lithuania
- The Ukraine
- Georgia
- Finland.

All of these territories gained a form of independence, initially as German protectorates. This handing over of land amounted to Russia's loss of:
- one-third of agricultural land
- one-third of all railway track
- one-third of the population of the Soviet Republic (about 55 million people)
- two-thirds of coal mines and half of heavy industry (iron and steel)
- nearly all available oil and most cotton textile production.

Lenin knew these conditions were harsh, but there is evidence he believed the war would soon be over, that Germany would be defeated and that territory would be recovered.

The consequences of the Treaty

The Treaty impacted on Russia in a number of ways:
- The departure of Bukharin and the Left SRs from the Soviet government meant that the Bolsheviks were in sole control of Russia.
- Once the burden of war had been lifted, the Bolsheviks started to implement their policies, often using repression – for example, the Cheka were used to arrest and punish hoarders of grain.
- The Treaty had exacerbated the problem of food shortages – this was due to the loss of the Ukraine, a major food-producing area.
- Opponents of the Bolsheviks used the crisis of food shortages to gain support. This was coupled with attacks on senior Bolshevik members, including Lenin.

Thus, it appears that the Treaty partly added to the problems faced by the Bolsheviks and did not work quite in the way that Lenin intended.

! Simple essay style

Below is a sample exam question. Use your own knowledge, information on the opposite page and information from other parts of this section on the nature of Russian government to produce a plan for this question. Choose four general points and provide three pieces of specific information to support each general point. Once you have planned your essay, write the introduction and conclusion for the essay. The introduction should list the points to be discussed in the essay. The conclusion should summarise the key points and justify which point was the most important.

'The Treaty of Brest-Litovsk (1918) was the strongest indicator of the effectiveness of Russian leaders in dealing with foreign affairs in the period from 1855 to 1964.' How far do you agree?

i Turning assertion into argument

Below are a series of definitions, a sample exam question and two sample conclusions. One of the conclusions achieves a high mark because it contains an argument. The other achieves a lower mark because it contains only description and assertion. Identify which is which. The mark scheme on page 7 will help you.

- **Description:** a detailed account.
- **Assertion:** a statement of fact or an opinion which is not supported by a reason.
- **Reason:** a statement which explains or justifies something.
- **Argument:** an assertion justified with a reason.

To what extent did the Treaty of Brest-Litovsk transform the Russian Empire in the period from 1855 to 1964?

The Treaty of Brest-Litovsk did transform the Russian Empire, as Germany demanded land which contained valuable resources. Russia lost Poland, Estonia, Latvia, Lithuania, the Ukraine, Georgia and Finland. These territories gained a form of independence, to begin with as German protectorates. This handing over of land amounted to Russia's loss of one-third of agricultural land, one-third of all railway tracks, one-third of the population of the Soviet Republic (about 55 million people), two-thirds of coalmines and half of heavy industry (iron and steel), nearly all available oil and most cotton textile production. Therefore, the Empire was certainly transformed as it became smaller and contained fewer resources than when the tsars were in control.

In conclusion, the Treaty of Brest-Litovsk did transform the Russian Empire, as territory was ceded to Germany, much of which contained valuable natural resources. For example, the handing over of the Ukraine meant a loss of rich, fertile soil for the growing of crops at a time when there were food shortages. However, Lenin believed the war would be over shortly after the signing of the Treaty and that Germany would be defeated. The result would be a return of lost land and to pre-war geographical boundaries. Lenin was proved correct in his prediction — thus, the Treaty had only a temporary impact and was relatively insignificant in how the Empire was to transform over a longer period of time.

Expansion in Central Asia

By the start of the Second World War the Soviet government had influence over the following parts of Central Asia:

- Kazakhstan
- Turkmenistan
- Uzbekistan
- Kyrgyzstan
- Tajikistan
- Azerbaijan.

Motives for expansion and control

Much of the Central Asian territory had been taken into Russian control by the 1880s through the use of force. In contrast to the tsars, the communists consolidated their control in the region through more peaceful means – the formulation of constitutions, especially that of 1936 (see page 14). The main motives for expansion and control were uniform throughout the period:

- Central Asia was to provide living and working space for large numbers of peasants from European Russia.
- The region was developed for cotton cultivation to serve the raw material needs of the textile factories in European Russia.
- The Central Asian territories bordered Afghanistan, India and China, creating the prospect of further expansion and influence in these areas.

Russian policies towards Central Asia

Central Asia largely avoided Russification – the tsars and communists seemed to think that, given the complexity of societies there and the difficulties with communication and transport, Russification was not achievable (or desirable). However, other measures had to be carried out if Russian leaders were to achieve their goals.

- The Steppe Statute of 1891 was passed, which granted 40 acres of land to peasant settlers – enough to establish a successful farm unit (although it was of no use to the native nomadic peoples).
- In 1910 Stolypin pushed for even greater migration to the area to accommodate rising peasant demands for land in European Russia.
- Islam had evolved as a major religion in Central Asia. The tsars showed some respect for Muslim people. Under Nicholas II the All-Russian Muslim League appeared and gained representation in the first *Dumas* (although after the 1907 electoral law, Asian Muslim representation in the *Duma* was disallowed). Under the communists there was condemnation of any repression that Muslim people had experienced under the tsars and guarantees that their rights would be protected.
- From 1915 to 1917, the Russian government attempted to draw on peoples from Central Asia to help with the war effort. However, they were deemed, in general, not fit for combat duties and were given other jobs; this caused a 'conscription revolt' which indicated how sensitive the population of Central Asia was to over involvement of Russian rulers in their affairs.
- The more remote, harsh areas of Central Asia were still used as 'dumping grounds' for groups from other parts of the Soviet Union that were seen to require punishing. For example, the Crimean Tartars were deported to South Kazakhstan in 1945, having been accused of collaborating with Germany.
- In 1957 Khrushchev issued a decree titled 'On the Rehabilitation of Deported Peoples'. This allowed many groups who had been deported in the period from 1941 to 1945 to return to their homelands. Some groups were excluded though, such as the Volga Germans and Meskhetians.
- Khrushchev also involved himself in the affairs of Central Asia through his Virgin Lands scheme. As with the migration policies of the tsars, this did not go down well with indigenous peoples as they felt swamped by immigrants looking to take even more land.

Thus, Central Asia became a highly valued part of the Russian Empire and the Soviet Union but, unlike other regions under Russian influence, it was allowed to keep its identity.

Spectrum of importance

Below are a sample exam question and a list of general points which could be used to answer the question. Use your own knowledge and the information on the opposite page to reach a judgement about the importance of these general points to the question posed.

Write numbers on the spectrum below to indicate their relative importance. Having done this, write a brief justification of your placement, explaining why some of these factors are more important than others. The resulting diagram could form the basis of an essay plan.

'Russian leaders showed interest in Central Asia in the period from 1855 to 1964 only for strategic reasons.' How far do you agree?

1 Control of Central Asia meant a protective buffer was created against China, Afghanistan and India.

2 Control of Central Asia meant the region could be used as a launch pad for incursions further east.

3 Important raw materials were to be found in Central Asia.

4 Central Asia provided extra living and working space for a growing Russian population.

5 Central Asia was viewed by Russian leaders as a recruitment ground for soldiers during times of war.

6 Criminals, dissidents and undesirables were deported to Central Asia.

Least important ⟷ Most important

RAG – Rate the timeline ⓐ

Below are a sample exam question and a timeline. Read the question, study the timeline and, using three coloured pens, put a red, amber or green star next to the events to show:

- Red: Events and policies that have no relevance to the question
- Amber: Events and policies that have some significance to the question
- Green: Events and policies that are directly relevant to the question

To what extent were the policies of the tsars and communist leaders towards Central Asia influenced by Russia's involvement in wars in the period from 1855 to 1964?

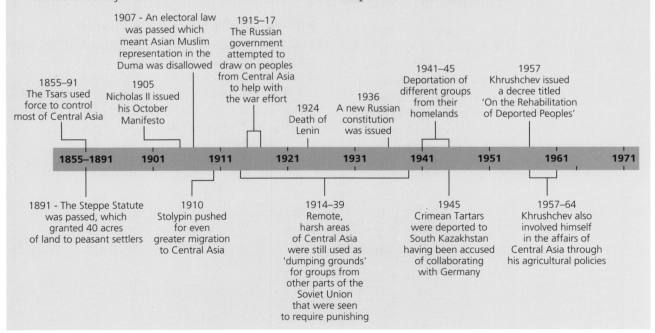

Expansion in the Far East

Background to the spread of Russian influence

Attempts to spread Russian influence in the Far East were largely governed by developments in transport and communications. Before the completion of the Trans-Siberian railway in 1903 the main route towards the Pacific coast was a dirt track. By the end of the nineteenth century it could still take up to three months to travel from Moscow to Sakhalin.

After the Russo–Japanese War, Russian involvement in the Far East was influenced mainly by further wars and conflicts. The First World War, the Russian Revolution and the Russian Civil War diverted the attention of Russian leaders from issues in the Far East. After the end of the Civil War, the communists returned to the region to address issues related to spheres of influence, occupation and conflict.

China

The relationship between Russia and China after the First World War was influenced by the following:

- From 1917 to 1937 the Chinese government was dominated by the **Kuomintang** (KMT) which, although not totally supportive of communism, was happy to accept support from Lenin and Stalin.
- After 1925 the KMT under **General Chiang Kai-shek** ordered the 'extermination' of trouble makers – communists, trade unionists and peasant leaders. Further purges happened in 1930 and 1934 – under their leader, Mao Zedong, the Chinese communists fought back against Chiang. The conflict was temporarily halted by the outbreak of war with Japan in 1937.
- The Soviet Union continued to support the KMT and helped Chiang resist Japanese advances.
- After the defeat of Japan at the end of the Second World War, fighting between the KMT and Chinese Communist Party resumed – Chiang's forces proved no match for the Chinese communists. In 1949 Mao gained control of the whole of mainland China. In October 1949 the People's Republic of China was created, with Mao as its leader.

Although the Soviets had supported the KMT, Mao initially acknowledged the hegemony (leadership) of Stalin when it came to attempts to spread communism in the post-war era. Until Stalin's death, relations between the two remained cordial. Under Khrushchev the friendship rapidly deteriorated – by the 1960s border disputes were emerging. The 'honeymoon period' between China and Russia ended.

Manchuria

From 1905 to 1931 Manchuria was under Japanese influence, and then from 1931 to 1945 the Japanese went further and occupied the territory. This meant control over Port Arthur, a base that would be of strategic importance to the Japanese. In 1945 Soviet troops liberated Manchuria and Stalin handed it back to China. However, the Soviet Union kept jurisdiction of Port Arthur until the death of Stalin in 1953.

Korea

Korea came under Japanese control in 1910. With the defeat of Japan in 1945 Korea was divided into two zones – the North (the area above the 38th parallel) was to be overseen by Russia and the South by the US. Disputes over possible reunification and who might rule a 'new' Korea led to war between the North and South. Matters were resolved in July 1953; a dividing line was established at the 38th parallel. The Soviet Union played no direct role in the war but it was still blamed by the US president, Truman, for influencing the initial invasion by the North. This heightened Cold War tensions and undoubtedly encouraged Khrushchev to introduce his policy of 'peaceful co-existence'.

Sinkiang, Tanu Tuva and Mongolia

Russian influence was also strong in regions to the north and north-west of China, especially Sinkiang province (north-west of China), Tanu Tuva (north of Mongolia) and Mongolia. As with other regions, the peoples in these areas had mixed success in attempting to break away from Soviet (and Chinese) influence.

Eliminate irrelevance

Below are a sample exam question and a paragraph written in answer to this question. Read the paragraph and identify parts of the paragraph that are not directly relevant to the question. Draw a line through the information that is irrelevant and justify your deletions in the margin.

To what extent were Russian attitudes towards expansion in the Far East a result of political changes in China in the period from 1855 to 1964?

Russian expansion in the Far East was partly driven by political changes in China during the stated period. However, this was mainly after 1925 when the ruling party in China, the Kuomintang (KMT), started to victimise the Chinese communists. Russia tolerated this up to and throughout the Second World War as the KMT led by Chiang Kai-shek was able to resist the advances of the Japanese. Russia's attitude towards expansion at this point was to hold fire until war was over and observe how relations between political groups in China unfolded. Also worth noting is that from 1905 to 1931 Manchuria was under Japanese influence and then from 1931 to 1945 the Japanese went further and occupied this territory. After the defeat of Japan at the end of the Second World War, fighting between the KMT and communists resumed — Chiang's forces proved no match for the Chinese communists. In 1949 Mao gained control of the whole of mainland China. In October 1949 the People's Republic of China was created, with Mao as its leader. Although the Soviets had supported the KMT, Mao initially acknowledged the hegemony (leadership) of Stalin when it came to attempts to spread communism in the post-war era. Until Stalin's death relations between the two remained cordial; Russia's attitude towards expansionism in the Far East up to 1953 was that it was not appropriate or relevant when it came to Chinese territory. Under Khrushchev the friendship rapidly deteriorated, though — by the 1960s border disputes between Russia and China were emerging, suggesting that Russia was changing its stance on expansionism.

Introducing and concluding an argument

Look at the key points of the answer below. How good is the proposed introduction? How effective is the proposed conclusion? Could either be improved – especially in relation to high-level answers?

'Russian expansion in the Far East in the period from 1855 to 1964 was very limited.' How far do you agree?

Key points:

- Limited with respect to time and place
- Manchuria: attempts to expand influence through occupation
- China: indirect influence
- North and north-west China: some influence
- Korea: indirect influence.

Introduction

Russian expansion in the Far East during the period concerned was limited to attempts at influencing the governance of states through the transmission of communist ideology. Physical expansion (that is, the taking of territory) was virtually non-existent, although there were times when Russian troops were placed in control of some Far Eastern regions. Overall, Russian expansion in the Far East was limited but mainly in terms of type of expansion, the timing of it and where it occurred.

Conclusion

Russian expansion in the Far East was limited with respect to its nature, timing and location. Expansion came mainly in the form of indirect influence over how governments in the Far East were organised, as opposed to the direct annexation of territory. Also, expansion was limited with respect to time; most attempts occurred after the construction of the Trans-Siberian railway in 1903 and then fell away after the mid-1950s.

Communist advances into Eastern and Central Europe after the Second World War

Stalin's motives

There are two main views about what motivated Stalin to influence how Central and Eastern Europe was to be governed after the Yalta conference.

- Stalin's policy was and is often viewed as one of expansionism.
- Another view is that by influencing the nature of government in neighbouring states Stalin would be protecting Russian interests – Central and Eastern countries would act as a kind of buffer against Western interference.

Stalin interfered in the governance of a number of Central and Eastern European countries by supporting the installation of pro-communist regimes. In some cases, such as with Hungary, free elections were put in place. However, such elements of democracy were limited by threats of force and imprisonment if voters and politicians did not toe the Soviet line. For example, elections in Hungary saw the communists gain just 20 per cent of votes, but they still managed to dominate the cabinet. Similar situations arose in Poland (see page 62), Bulgaria, Albania and Romania; by the end of 1947 all of these states had communist governments.

The extent of Russian influence

The table below gives a summary of how individual Central and Eastern European states were affected.

State	Extent of Russian influence
Yugoslavia	In 1945 elections were held in Yugoslavia. The outcome was the installation of a communist government led by Marshal Tito. Tito wanted to continue consolidating Yugoslavian autonomy and therefore resisted attempts by Stalin to interfere. He objected to the over-centralisation of government of Stalinism and introduced his own brand of communism. Tito kept Yugoslavia free from direct Soviet control until his death in 1980.
Czechoslovakia	After the Second World War free elections were held in Czechoslovakia (1946). They resulted in the formation of coalition government consisting mainly of left-wing parties, including communists. Just before new elections, scheduled for May 1948, the communists in Czechoslovakia seized power. This resulted in the resignation of most non-communist members of the coalition. The elections proceeded but were rigged; under Russian guidelines voters were given a list of candidates to vote for, all of whom were communists.
Hungary	As with other East European states, 'free' elections were held in Hungary at the end of the Second World War but, despite gaining less than one-fifth of the votes, Hungarian communists ended up dominating the cabinet. Clearly, Stalin had influenced the setting up of the new regime. However, the Hungarian communists were not all pro-Stalin and protested; by the end of 1949 nearly a quarter of a million party members had been expelled. Until Stalin's death, Hungary was governed repressively by the Stalinist Matyas Rakosi. Khrushchev's de-Stalinisation gave hope to Hungarians that positive change would occur, but by October 1956 disquiet at the slow pace of reform led to a major uprising. This was dealt with ruthlessly by the Soviet regime.
East Germany	At Yalta, the 'Four Power Control of Zones' principle was established; Russia was given temporary jurisdiction over the eastern part of Germany. This agreement was undermined by a number of developments: Stalin's statement in 1946 that 'all Germany must be ours'; the creation of Bizonia; the introduction of the Deutschmark and Ostmark; the Berlin Blockade (1948–49); the approval of the West German constitution. These events led to the USSR officially 'creating' East Germany in October 1949.
Others	In Poland, Romania, Bulgaria and Albania, monarchies were abolished and communist governments established, all by the end of 1947. Of the Balkan states, Greece was an exception – there, the communists were easily defeated.

Develop the detail

Below are a sample exam question and a paragraph written in answer to this question. The paragraph contains a limited amount of detail. Annotate the paragraph to add additional detail to the answer.

'The Soviet Union's expansion into Central and Eastern Europe after the Second World War was the only time in the period from 1855 to 1964 when Russian leaders were successful in influencing the governance of other countries.' How far do you agree?

Russian leaders were certainly successful in influencing the governments of a number of Central and Eastern European states from 1945 to the mid-1950s. Most of this influence came in the form of transmission of ideology and the military backing of regimes that agreed to adopt Soviet-style communism. However, some Central and Eastern European countries were successful in resisting Soviet control. Also, this was not the only time in the period from 1855 to 1964 that Russian leaders were successful in influencing the governance of other countries.

 Recommended reading

Below is a list of suggested further reading on this topic.

- Edward Acton, *Russia: The Tsarist and Soviet Legacy* (1995)
- Martin Gilbert, *The Routledge Atlas of Russian History* (fourth edition, 2007)
- Andrew Holland, *Russia and its Rulers 1855–1964* (second edition, 2016)
- Stephen J. Lee, *Russia and the USSR, 1855–1991* (2005)
- Dominic Lieven, *Towards the Flame* (2015)
- Geoffrey Roberts, *The Soviet Union in World Politics* (1999)

Exam focus

Below is a sample high-level essay. Read the response and the comments around it.

'The armistice of 1920 was the most important turning point in Russo-Polish relations from 1855 to 1964.' How far do you agree?

The relative importance of turning points in Russo-Polish relations from 1855 to 1964 can be measured by making reference to how they engendered political, economic and social change. The 1920 armistice was undoubtedly significant as the freedom and territory gained were to remain in place until immediately after the Second World War. However, there were other events that resulted in substantial change, namely the 1863 Polish Revolt, the rise of socialism in Poland in the 1890s, the rise of Nazism, the wartime conferences at Yalta and Potsdam and the change in leadership of Russia in the mid-1950s. Out of all of these, Yalta and Potsdam stand out as creating the greatest 'turn' as they paved the way for a sustained period of control by Russia over Poland, putting an end to independence gained in 1920.

The Russo-Polish conflict of 1920 ended on 16 October 1920 when an armistice between the two warring states was signed. Politically, for Poland, this was something of a turning point as Polish independence was confirmed and it was agreed that Western Ukraine and Western Belorussia should come under Polish authority. This was an acknowledgement from the Bolsheviks that Poland could not be defeated militarily and could hold its own as a political power. In contrast, the attempt by rebels in 1863 to gain political independence failed; the Milyutin reforms resulted in the exile of hundreds of members of the Polish nobility to Siberia and the transfer of their estates to incoming Russian officials who were to take over their duties. This marked the start of the Russification of Poland: the level of nationalism diminished along with the level of autonomy that the Poles had experienced before the revolt. Russification ensured that, until the end of 1915, Poland was considered an integral part of Russia. Although there was some challenge to Russification in the 1890s with the rise of Socialism in Poland and the appointment of Poles to the first and second *Dumas*, this was short-lived. A greater degree of political change resulted from the Yalta and Potsdam wartime conferences in the 1940s. The Yalta and Potsdam agreements over what was to happen to Poland paved the way for Russia to implement fully a Soviet-style government across the territory of the newly reconstituted country. By 1952, with the imposition of a Soviet-style constitution, Poland was officially renamed the People's Republic of Poland – a situation which lasted until 1989. Thus, Yalta and Potsdam were politically the most important events as they resulted in a sustained period of Russian control over the governance and administration of Poland.

With respect to economic independence, the 1920 armistice had a positive effect on Poland; it gained territory containing valuable natural resources and the autonomy to develop its own industry and trading partners. In comparison, the 1863 Polish Revolt also had positive economic repercussions especially for peasants as, under Russian administration, they gained their freedom to grow whatever crops they wanted, on their own allotments. In the 1890s, with the formation of the Polish Socialist Party (PPS) in 1892 and the Social Democratic Party in 1893, there was also some improvement in the economic conditions for workers; the two pressure groups were able to challenge authorities to provide workers with higher wages and shorter hours. This was similar to the emergence of the Stalinist-influenced Polish Workers' Party (PPR), which was formed to promote the rights of communist workers. However, by August 1948 the PPR was the only party that could be voted for (thus, a one-party state had been established). Those who questioned the lack of freedom that emerged, such as members of the Church and trade unions, were arrested. After the Yalta and Potsdam conferences, Russian authority over all economic matters in Poland was firmly established, including how the economy was planned and operated and how workers' rights were to be restricted.

A solid introduction that gives an indication of how the importance of possible turning points is to be measured and what events are to be discussed. There is also clear indication of the line of argument that is to be followed.

This section provides evidence of synthesis and the development of a synoptic argument. Some very sound links and comparisons are made, with a sustained focus on Russo-Polish relations.

A different theme of independence is considered here. The argument about Yalta and Potsdam being the most important turning point is built on. Maybe something could have been said about Khrushchev's policies towards Poland and its economy.

With respect to social independence, the 1920 armistice had a limited impact; the gaining of Western Ukraine and Western Belorussia changed the ethnic composition of Poland but, in general, Polish traditions, values and institutions remained. This was very different from what had happened after the 1863 Polish Revolt, when Russification resulted in Russian becoming the official language of administration and governance and the Catholic Church not being allowed to communicate with the Vatican in an attempt to diminish its authority (it was believed that a number of bishops had been sympathetic to the rebels). In the 1890s, the emergence of a Polish proletariat altered the social structure but, despite gaining independence in 1918 via the Brest-Litovsk Treaty and having this reinforced by the 1920 armistice, Poland's control over how its society was to be managed was short-lived. The rise of Hitler and his Lebensraum policy, the Nazi-Soviet Pact of 1939 and the course of the Second World War all combined to have a negative impact on Polish society. The Yalta and Potsdam agreements were again pivotal in that they led to Soviet control over all aspects of Polish life, including institutions such as schools and hospitals. There was some easing of repression by Khrushchev – for example, peasants were allowed to leave collective farms to set up independent smallholdings and the Catholic Church was once more allowed to teach religion in schools. Generally, though, Polish society remained under the influence of Soviet policies and values until 1989.

The armistice between Poland and Russia signed in October 1920 was an important turning point in Russo-Polish relations from 1855 to 1964. Under the agreement, Polish independence was confirmed and the freedom and territory gained in 1920 was to remain in place until immediately after the Second World War. This was the longest period of Polish independence from Russian control across the whole period. In contrast, the 1863 Polish Revolt led to Russification and less Polish autonomy, freedoms granted under the Treaty of Brest-Litovsk were not consolidated until the end of the Civil War and Hitler's Lebensraum policy only affected Polish sovereignty from 1939 until 1945. However, more important than the 1920 armistice were the conferences at Yalta and Potsdam in 1945. They laid a foundation for Russia to sovietise Eastern Europe, including Poland. Despite Khrushchev's easing of repression of Poland, it remained a satellite state of Russia until 1989. Thus, in comparison to the 1920 armistice, the conferences of 1945 had a greater long-term and negative impact, from a Polish point of view, on Russo-Polish relations.

There is some lack of explanation and support here (for example, over the importance of the events of the 1930s) but in general, the answer continues to show synthesis and synopsis and covers the whole period. This is a clear indication that the answer would need to be placed in one of the higher levels of the generic mark scheme.

A very good conclusion that is very much in line with the argument that is developed in the main body of the essay. A clear judgement has been reached – note that this is based on the view that 1945 was the most important turning point due to the negative impact that it had on Polish autonomy. Remember that turning points do not necessarily constitute positive change.

Overall, a clearly structured, well-focused and sustained answer. The essay reveals an ability to synthesise a range of material over the whole period before arriving at a judgement on the issue concerned. The answer lacks some development (for example, there is little mention of the unrest in Poland in the early 1950s) and support in places but it does go beyond a narrative, descriptive-based approach or one that merely lists potential points without making comparisons. Thus, the essay would reach a reasonably high level.

Moving towards Level 6

Use the comments and the mark scheme in order to move the response to the very top of Level 6, making a list of the additional features that would enable the answer to achieve full marks. Remember it does not have to be a perfect answer, but one that best fits with the descriptors.

5 Depth study: Alexander II's domestic reforms

Key debate 1: How 'liberal' was Russian government from 1855 to 1881?

Changes to government

The main area of debate with respect to the rule of Alexander II is the extent to which the reforms he carried out genuinely granted liberty (freedom) to the peoples of Russia. Traditionally he was viewed as the 'Tsar Liberator', mainly as a result of the Emancipation Edict of 1861 and its consequences. There are some historians, such as J. N. Westwood, who have perpetuated the view that Alexander II intentionally carried out reforms that granted Russians greater freedoms so that they could live better lives. Hence, Westwood believes that 'with the possible exceptions of Khrushchev and Gorbachev, no Russian ruler brought so much relief to so many of his people as did Alexander II, autocratic and conservative though he was'.

Others, though, have emphasised the limitations of the reforms to argue that the tsar was concerned only with making some concessions to win support. Despite being labelled the 'Tsar Liberator' there is some consensus among historians that Alexander II never wavered from being an autocrat. The tsar made only one, relatively minor, change to the offices of government – the Personal Chancellery of his Imperial Majesty was abolished in 1861 and replaced with a Council of Ministers.

Changes to local government

More contentious were the reforms made to local government. The significance of the *Zemstva* (see page 16) is debated for the following reasons.

- Some historians have claimed that once the emancipation of the serfs occurred then local government had to change.
- The tsar was forced to introduce an element of democracy at local level but then seemed to regret this immediately. Liberal members of the *Zemstva* started to question the 'administrative monopoly of officialdom' and were critical of a regime that was perceived to be unresponsive to their demands.

- Both the district and provincial *Zemstva* were dominated by the nobility. The extent to which democracy was introduced is questionable. Also, the creation of the *Zemstva* appeared to divert the attention of the reformist nobility away from wanting changes to central government.
- Writers who appear sympathetic towards Russian tsarism have emphasised the successes of the *Zemstva*. For example, they did much 'good work' in the fields of education, public health and local economies. The original *Zemstva* were seen as so effective that, from 1870 onwards, the model was copied and applied to towns and cities.

Opposition to Alexander II

There is no doubt that opposition to Alexander did increase, partly due to the more liberal climate he created, but whether this meant that his assassination was then a certainty is open to debate.

The historian Orlando Figes believes that opposition to Alexander II occurred logically as a result of his reforms. He claims that:

- The creation of *Zemstva* resulted in the emergence of the Populist movement.
- When the Populists failed, in the 'mad summer' of 1874, some of them turned to 'revolutionary terror' to gain support from peasants. This splinter group (the People's Will) turned to 'assassinating government officials in the hope that, if they weakened the autocracy, the peasantry would join them in revolt'.
- Four attempts were made to assassinate the tsar. It was only a matter of time before one succeeded (1 March 1881).

Not all agree with this – for example, the historian Geoffrey Hosking has questioned whether the Populists were unsuccessful. He believes that 'going to the people' resulted in a significant number of peasant groups being encouraged to 'share some of the radicals' ideas, for example about egalitarianism in landholding'. Thus, it was not necessarily inevitable that the tsar's liberal reforms, plus the failures of the Populists, led to Alexander II's assassination.

! Interpretations: content or argument? ⓐ

Read the following interpretation and the two alternative answers to the question.

Which answer focuses more on the content and which one focuses more on the arguments of the interpretation? Explain your choice.

> Using your understanding of the historical context, assess how convincing the arguments in this extract are in relation to Alexander II's motives for making the Emancipation Proclamation (1861).

The interpretation claims that the Emancipation Edict was just one part of an overall programme for reform. It states that the reforms were carried out so that peasants would not rebel. The tsar had said it was better to reform from above than allow it to occur from below. In other words, if the government took the initiative and provided the peasants with what they wanted, they would be less likely to revolt. Also, the reforms meant that Russia would have a fitter workforce and army to help it catch up with the West.

The interpretation argues that Alexander II's reforms were carried out mainly to prevent the likelihood of rebellion from peasants. This can be supported by the fact that in 1856 the tsar famously claimed that 'it is better to begin abolishing serfdom from above than to wait for it to abolish itself from below'. Indeed, as the interpretation points out, the number of peasant revolts before the mid-1850s was increasing and, given the extra challenges posed by the Crimean War, there was a real chance that tsarist autocracy would be under threat. The interpretation also points out that the reforms may have been designed for the purposes of efficiency; a healthier and better educated population would have resulted in Russia strengthening its status. However, this view underplays the magnitude of the tsar's reforms as a whole. He knew that emancipation would be just one strand that formed a package and that together this would have brought relief to peasants on a scale that no other Russian leader was able to do in the period from 1855 to 1964.

INTERPRETATION

Adapted from Michael Lynch, History Today *(published in* History Review, *Issue 47, December 2003).*

Alexander II's motives for introducing the Emancipation Proclamation (1861)

Emancipation proved the first in a series of measures that Alexander produced as a part of a programme that included legal and administrative reform and the extension of press and university freedoms. But behind all these reforms lay an ulterior motive. Alexander II was not being liberal for its own sake. According to official records kept by the Ministry of the Interior (equivalent to the Home Office in Britain) there had been 712 peasant uprisings in Russia between 1826 and 1854. By granting some of the measures that the intelligentsia had called for, while in fact tightening control over the peasants, Alexander intended to lessen the social and political threat to the established system that those figures frighteningly represented. Above all, he hoped that an emancipated peasantry, thankful for the gifts that a bountiful tsar had given them, would provide physically fitter and morally worthier recruits for Russia's armies, the symbol and guarantee of Russia's greatness as a nation.

Key debate 2: To what extent did reforms made by Alexander II improve the status of Russian peasants?

REVISED

The impact of the Emancipation Edict (1861) on Russian peasants

The Emancipation Edict was the most important measure enacted by Alexander II, as from this other economic, social and political changes became a necessity. The impact of the stipulations of the Edict has been much discussed by historians. The conditions laid down by the Edict were as follows:

- All privately owned serfs were freed. Those kept by the state were to be emancipated in 1866. Freedom entailed peasants being able to own property, run their own commercial enterprises and marry whomever they wished.
- Nobles had to hand over a proportion or allotment of land to peasants. This was measured and allocated by official surveyors.
- The state provided compensation to landowners, which was often based on valuations way above the market level.
- Peasants had to help pay for the compensation through redemption payments (that is, repayments of loans that allowed peasants to make the compensation). These were to be paid over a 49-year period at six per cent interest. Legal rights to the land were only confirmed after the last payment was made. An alternative was for peasants to continue to work on the land of a noble for a certain number of days in a year to compensate for their own land allocations.
- The administration of redemption payments was carried out by the village council of elders (the *mir*). This group also ensured that land could not be sold on before the final redemption payment had been made.

Opposition from landowners

The reform, taken at face value, would justify Alexander II being given the title of 'Liberator'. It has been described as 'an enormous step forward' – as well as their freedom, peasants also acquired their own parcel of land. But it has often been pointed out that there was considerable opposition to the statute from landowners, even though the compensation clauses did much to allay their fears. The main reason for this was that the nobility had been struggling to maintain their large estates before emancipation. Many had taken out large loans to help cover day-to-day costs. The revenue from redemption payments tended to be diverted to repay debts. If this failed, estates were broken up and sold off. Thus, by 1905, the land owned by the nobility had been reduced by about 40 per cent.

Opposition from peasants

Many peasants also reacted badly to the reform for the following reasons:

- Generally, peasants were allocated poorer-quality land. They also received less land, on average, than they had been farming before emancipation.
- Many peasants struggled to earn enough from the land to meet redemption payments. Financial difficulties were made worse by the necessity to pay rural poll taxes.
- Peasants were not totally free insofar as they had to answer to the *mir* – decisions about what was to be produced and how crops were to be cultivated still had to be made by the village elders. It was also the responsibility of the *mir* to ensure that the principle of subsistence farming was adhered to. As a result, the more able peasant farmers had no incentive to produce surpluses and were reluctant to invest to improve the land.

Thus, it would seem that the freedoms given to peasants were rather limited – this remained the case throughout Alexander II's reign.

! Using knowledge to support or contradict a

Below is a passage to read. You are asked to summarise the interpretation about the impact of the Emancipation Edict (1861) on Russian peasants and then offer a counter-argument based on the interpretation and your own knowledge.

Interpretation offered by the source:

_____

_____

Counter-argument:

_____

_____

_____

_____

PASSAGE A

From Peter Oxley, Russia 1855–1991: From Tsars to Commissars _(2001), page 27._

The peasants now had less land than they had before, and were having to pay a redemption tax higher than the land was worth. The landowner often reserved the best land for himself. When the growth of population is taken into account, and the redistribution of the land which inevitably followed this increase, land shortage became an ever increasing problem, leaving peasant families helpless if the harsh Russian climate was worse than usual. A sign of the economic difficulties facing many peasants was the growing amount of redemption and poll tax arrears, a feature for the next 20 years. There was no incentive for a peasant family to invest in their land, if it could be taken from them and reallocated when the village population expanded. Most peasants continued to farm in the same inefficient ways as before.

How far do you agree?

Read the following passage.

Summarise each of its arguments. Use your knowledge to agree or contradict.

Argument in extract	Knowledge that corroborates	Knowledge that contradicts
1.		
2.		
3.		

PASSAGE B

From Jonathan Bromley, Russia 1848–1917 _(2002), page 177._

Emancipation was gradual. Serfs were 'temporarily bound' for ten years and redemption dues were stretched out over 49 years. With hindsight, this seems overly conservative. But it is hard to argue that the emancipation of the serfs had been anything other than successful from the perspective of 1881. Above all, considering the number of people involved (some 22 million families) and the unprecedented nature of the reform, emancipation went ahead with remarkably little disruption. It was followed by 20 years of rising yields and improved efficiency. Finally, we must be aware of the state's financial limitations with regard to emancipation. Giving vast loans to the peasantry to speed up land transfer was quite unrealistic in the difficult financial conditions that followed the Crimean War.

Key debate 3: How far were Alexander II's reforms due to the Crimean War?

The Crimean War is often cited as being the chief reason behind the issuing of the Emancipation Edict of 1861 and other reforms that followed this. The causal link is based on the following observations:

- The war revealed weaknesses in the way Nicholas I had ruled; the maintenance of serfdom under strict autocratic rule did not seem to fit with staging modern warfare.
- The army was recruited from serfs who were not trained to the same standard as the professional armies of Britain and France. Also, serfs were inclined towards revolt and, given their other responsibilities, were probably not as committed as they might have been.
- Soldiers had been poorly supplied; the production of armaments and uniforms was inadequate. This was a reflection on the way the economy was organised and how Russia had been slow to industrialise.

However, the causal link between the Crimean War and Alexander II's reforms is questionable – correlation is no proof of causation. Some historians have pointed out that there were other reasons for Alexander II's reforms, some of which were linked to what had happened in Russia before the Crimean War. These included:

- pressure to abolish serfdom, as it was seen by some as a form of slavery and an institution that was immoral
- growing peasant unrest that could be traced back to the 1770s
- demands from some politicians and entrepreneurs for more labour to work on projects such as railway routes
- population growth, which put pressure on a farming system that was geared up to provide subsistence and not surplus. Famines became more frequent as the demand for food outstripped supply.

Thus, arguing that the Crimean War was the main reason for Alexander II's reforms is misleading. It was one of a number of factors that influenced change.

Given the failures of the Russian military during the war it is not surprising that Alexander II prioritised major reforms. How far-reaching and effective these reforms were has been a matter of debate:

- Although aspects of the reforms, such as conscription and the reduction in periods of service, were seen as radical, as a package weaknesses were revealed. For example, new training regimes were compromised by the poor level of education of recruits (although this was eventually addressed through the establishment of military schools).
- The historian John Hite has emphasised that in 1877 the Russian army struggled to defeat 'weak Turkish troops' and later, in 1904–05, Russia was beaten by Japan.
- The reforms were slow to come about; some nobles were only convinced of the need for far-reaching reforms when they witnessed the success of the 'modern' Prussian army in 1866–71.

Some commentators have suggested that it is easy to be critical of the military reorganisation programme with the benefit of hindsight. At the time, the tsar and other senior members of the aristocracy appeared confident that the reforms would aid the modernisation of Russia. The economic costs of supporting an ineffective standing army were reduced, agricultural efficiency was improved (peasants had more freedom and time to work on the land), soldiers were better trained, and, in the long run, there was an improvement in literacy. Therefore, in context, the military reforms were more radical than some observers have made out.

Quick quizzes at **www.hoddereducation.co.uk/myrevisionnotes**

Read the following interpretation and the two alternative answers to the question.

Which answer focuses more on the content and which one focuses more on the arguments of the interpretation? Explain your choice.

> Using your understanding of the historical context, assess how convincing the arguments in this passage are in relation to an analysis of the influence of the Crimean War on Alexander II's reforms.

Stephen J. Lee states that the Crimean War did influence Alexander II to make reforms. Russia performed badly in the war, which prompted the tsar to carry out reforms to the military that related to recruitment, leadership and administration. Other reforms had to follow, such as the emancipation of serfs in 1861 and those to local government. Stephen J. Lee also highlights why Alexander II carried out these reforms: he wanted to strengthen autocracy and improve Russia's standing in the world.

The argument put forward in the interpretation about the impact of the Crimean War on Russian domestic policy has some validity in that it highlights how the conflict was both a cause and effect of changes that were made to the way Russia was ruled. The tsar's military reforms were the first to be put in place (and were reinforced later in his reign), which suggests that Russia's poor showing in the war was a great concern and immediate measures were deemed necessary to help prevent a repeat of this in the future. Also, as the recruitment for the military had been based on aspects of serfdom, it was logical for the tsar to turn to the emancipation issue after he had dealt with more specific military issues. The war, therefore, gave reason for reform but, as the interpretation points out, the outcome of the conflict was an effect of an outdated military system and medieval serfdom. However, the argument is undermined by the fact that Nicholas I had considered making reforms, in particular the abolition of serfdom. His motive had little to do with the war. As acknowledged by his son, peasant revolt had become a serious issue before the war and the tsarist regime was starting to believe that it was better to reform from above than allow change to be instigated from below. Thus, the interpretation places too much emphasis on the war as a motive for reform.

PASSAGE

From Stephen J. Lee, Russia and the USSR, 1855–1991 *(2006), pages 118–19.*

The influence of the Crimean War on Alexander II's reforms

The Crimean War was both a reason for and an effect of key adjustments in Tsarist policy on autocracy. The first of these was the decision of Alexander II, immediately after his accession in 1855, to introduce major reforms, even though Nicholas I had generally resisted change. A key factor was Russia's poor performance in the Crimean War (1854-56), a reflection on the recruiting system, the military leadership, the supply chain and the bureaucratic inefficiency. The result was a series of reforms, beginning with the emancipation of the serfs in 1861 and proceeding to the updating of local government (1864 and 1870), changes in military organisation and the recruiting system (1874) and improvements in education. Such developments were intended to strengthen, not weaken the autocratic base; they also increased Alexander II's awareness of Russia's advantages as a modernised power against its traditional rival – the Ottoman Empire.

Key debate 4: How far were issues relating to the Empire and minorities neglected by Alexander II?

REVISED

Many of the well-known texts on tsarist Russia pay scant attention to the impact of the reign of Alexander II on the Russian Empire and minorities. There appears to be an underlying assumption that the tsar's domestic reforms affected all of the Empire in a similar way. A good example is the emancipation of serfs. Some historians give the impression that a Russian peasant was the same kind of rural worker regardless of the region and time in which they lived.

The impact of Alexander II's domestic reforms

Alexander II's domestic reforms are usually analysed with respect to how successful they were in achieving their aims. Most discussion revolves around the connection between the Emancipation Edict and reforms that followed, especially reforms to regional government. The break-up of serfdom took away authority from the nobility to administer and govern at a local level. As a result:

● The introduction of the *Zemstva* to take over the running of local affairs is seen as a major step towards liberalising the Empire.
● Some historians have pointed out some of the long-term failings of the *Zemstva*, though few have paid attention to how they were viewed in particular parts of the Empire and by minorities.

Alexander II and Poland

It is not always clear exactly how significant an impact the tsar's reforms had on particular places. This is especially true of Poland.

● The Polish rebellion of 1863 was the result of the complex interplay of factors including the access to land, the proposed policies of the Polish leaders, Mikhail Gorchakov and Alexander Wielopolski, and the role of the Catholic Church in Polish society.
● Alexander II tried very hard to compromise with the Polish government by allowing them to frame their own land reform programme.
● Extremists in Poland opposed the proposals (along with those related to conscription) and rebellion erupted.
● Of particular note is that peasants divided their allegiance – some supported the insurgents while others backed the Russians.
● After the rebellion was ruthlessly suppressed in 1864 the tsar imposed reforms which benefited the majority of peasants to the detriment of the nobility.

The Polish rebellion was quite obviously the start of the Russification process (although this is usually attributed to Alexander III). This supports the argument that Alexander II was very concerned to maintain order across the whole of the Empire.

Alexander II and other regions

The tsar showed concern for most peoples of the Empire.

● Other hints of 'separatism' that appeared after 1864 were given much attention. For example, an official commission was set up in 1876 to investigate separatist activity in the Ukraine.
● Alexander II continued his father's liberal policy towards the Baltic Germans (the upper-class peoples of Latvia and Estonia). This was done in the face of rising nationalism in both states, mainly from the middle-class intelligentsia.
● The tsar took some practical measures to improve the lot of Jewish people. For example, some categories of Jewish people (merchants and doctors, in particular) were allowed to live outside the Pale of Settlement.
● During the rule of Alexander II there was significant Russian expansion into Central Asia.

Alexander II was well aware of the need to monitor developments across the whole of the Empire in response to his programme of reforms. He also listened to the demands of national minorities and, in general, reacted in a responsible manner. It is therefore important to bear in mind the ethnic make-up of the Empire when evaluating the tsar's achievements.

! Using knowledge to support or contradict

Below is a passage to read. You are asked to summarise the interpretation about the impact of Alexander II's reforms on Poland and then develop a counter-argument.

Interpretation offered by the source:

_____

_____

Counter-argument:

_____

_____

_____

_____

PASSAGE

From Geoffrey Hosking, Russia and the Russians: From Earliest Times to 2001 *(2001), page 304.*

The Polish Rebellion of 1863

Right at the outset Alexander II's civic reforms faced a challenge in the most sensitive region of the empire. By restoring a degree of Polish autonomy, promoting the expansion of primary education, planning the reopening of Warsaw University, and encouraging public discussion of the emancipation of the serfs, Alexander stimulated the Polish elites to feel themselves once again the leaders of a potential nation. While some Poles, led by Marquis Alexander Wielopolski, believed it was in Poland's best interests to work with the Russian government to take reform further and regain Polish civic nationhood, others wanted to use the opportunity to move swiftly to full independence and the reclamation of the eastern territories in Lithuania and Belorussia which Poland had lost in the eighteenth century partitions.

⚡ How far do you agree?

Read the passage above once more. Summarise each of its arguments. Use your knowledge to agree or contradict.

Argument in extract	Knowledge that corroborates	Knowledge that contradicts
1.		
2.		
3.		

Exam focus

Below are a sample depth-study question on Alexander II's domestic reforms and an example of a high-level answer. Read the answer and the comments around it.

Evaluate the interpretations in both of the two passages and explain which you think is more convincing as an explanation of Alexander II's domestic policies.

PASSAGE A

Adapted from J. N. Westwood, Endurance and Endeavour: Russian History 1812–2001 *(2002), page 66.*

The main events of [Alexander II's] reign were, first and very foremost the freeing of the serfs; then, and partly in connection with this reform, real changes in local government, justice, education and the army. As so often happens, reform and relaxation were followed by protests, manifested notably by a revolutionary movement. The 'Tsar Emancipator' also had to cope with two burdens that had afflicted his father: cholera and the Poles. These trials led to reaction, and there was a partial return to tactics of repression. However, just before his assassination and having, as he thought, succeeded in calming the Empire, Alexander was considering a new series of reforms to relieve political pressures. Throughout the reign there was steady economic progress, expansion in Central Asia, some attempt to overcome the financial consequences of the Crimean War and a continuation of railway building.

PASSAGE B

Adapted from J. Grenville, Europe Reshaped *(1999), pages 262–63.*

In view of Alexander II's character – he was rather indolent and indecisive and despite public displays of emotion and kindheartedness capable of maintaining a severe police regime with all its attendant cruelties – it is surprising that it was especially his reign that became associated with the period of great reforms in Russian history. To the extent that in an autocracy good deeds are credited to the autocrat personally, he earned the title 'Tsar Liberator'. Nevertheless, his personal contribution to reforms was less positive than his more admiring biographers would have us believe. In many ways his influence impeded the practical realisation of reforms that had become law. He was indecisive and throughout his reign alternated between reforming impulses and reaction. As his advisers he selected both true reformers such as Dimitri Milyutin and extreme conservatives, men such as Dimitri Tolstoy, and kept both in office simultaneously. It was only with reluctance that Alexander took up the root cause of Russia's social ills, the problem of the serfs. Once a programme of emancipation had been devised, the other practical reforms of his reign followed from that.

The 'great reforms' of the 1860s did not liberate the Russian people. The process was so gradual, and the contrast between aspirations, the laws of the state and the realities of the situation were so stark, that the degree of discontent was raised more by the hope of reform than satisfied by their application.

Both passages give appropriate consideration to the importance of Alexander II's domestic reforms and, in particular, highlight how positive a move the emancipation of serfs was. However, they differ in terms of the amount of credit that is given to the tsar for the formulation and implementation of reforms. Passage A is very supportive of what Alexander II achieved whereas Passage B offers a more cynical view of the tsar's motives for reforming.

Passage A supports the traditional view that Alexander II was the 'Tsar Emancipator', starting with the claim that the emancipation of the serfs was the 'main event' of the reign; the Emancipation Edict of 1861 did indeed move Russia towards a modernising process, especially as it forced other political, social and economic reforms to take place. In general, Westwood paints a very positive account of the tsar's reign and stresses that if he had not been assassinated he would have gone on to make further changes (the most monumental of which would have been the introduction of constitutional rule). Passage A is convincing in that it places Alexander II's achievements in the context of the challenges he faced (the impact of the Crimean War, opposition, social problems such as cholera and the legacy of his father). However, less persuasive is the idea that the tsar was more benevolent than his father ('there was a partial return to tactics of repression'). Alexander II was first and foremost an autocratic tsar,' which is reflected in his view that the emancipation of serfs had to occur to prevent revolution (and not because it was an issue of equality and justice). Also, the fact that peasants had been rebelling before 1855 counters the claim that opposition only came to the fore when Alexander II relaxed his grip over the Russian people. Opposition existed throughout his reign; the Populist movement was a reflection of the culmination of resentment that had built up over decades and it was possibly a coincidence that it gained momentum at the time when the tsar made 'liberal' changes.

Passage B challenges the traditional view of Alexander II and claims that the tsar, through his innate conservatism, actually impeded the pace and extent of reform. Grenville gives little consideration to context, instead focusing on the personal qualities of the tsar. Passage B provides a strong case for the tsar being a reluctant reformer in his approach to dealing with the social condition of Russia, claiming that he and his advisers were not totally committed to reform. This was clearly indicated by their slowness to act. It was the case that it took Alexander II until 1861 to make the Emancipation Edict and that other major reforms did not appear until after that time. This time lag between Alexander taking power and reform coincided with opposition gathering momentum and attempts on the tsar's life. Against this argument, though, is that Alexander needed time to win over support from the aristocracy; major landowners had much to lose from emancipation and voiced their concerns when the reform had first been mooted by Nicholas I. Grenville's account would be more credible if it stressed the political, economic and social climate in which Alexander II found himself and how well he coped with the fall-out from the Crimean War.

On balance, Passage A is a slightly more convincing view of Alexander II's policies as it places them in context, highlights their achievements (in the domestic and foreign spheres) and implies that as a whole they represented progress. Passage B, in contrast, is less balanced and is more of a personal attack on the tsar, which masks the critical analysis that it attempts to develop.

Overall, the answer shows a good focus on the question. There is some awareness of the wider debate over the motives and achievements of Alexander II. Some contextual knowledge is deployed to evaluate the interpretations and reach a judgement. The answer is worthy of a mark in the higher levels of the mark scheme.

Evaluate the Interpretation

The key to a good answer is to evaluate the given Interpretation and use your own knowledge to show the strengths and limitations of the Interpretation. Go through the response and identify all the evaluative words that are used in the answer.

A sound observation is made about how both passages stress the importance of the emancipation of the serfs. The main contrast in the passages is also correctly identified.

This section provides a well-developed and clearly structured analysis of Passage A. It contains balanced comment and measures the validity of Westwood's claims against an appropriate amount of contextual knowledge.

These comments are also balanced and consider the strengths and limitations of Grenville's account. The paragraph seems to end in a stronger judgement of the validity of the explanation than is made of Passage A.

A clear judgement is made here; this conclusion is congruent with the rest of the answer and does not add any new analysis or detail.

6 Depth study: The Provisional Government

Key debate 1: To what extent was the Provisional Government doomed to fail from the start?

REVISED

The formation and tenure of the Provisional Government (March–October 1917) has caused much debate among historians. The main bone of contention is the extent to which the government failed.

- Some believe that the Provisional Government was doomed from the start but did not help itself by making poor decisions.
- Others argue that the new government was successful in achieving its main aim, which was the preparation for elections to a new Constituent Assembly.
- It was not so much the failings of the Provisional Government that led to the October Revolution of 1917, but the determination of the Bolsheviks to seize power.

Those who view the Provisional Government as an abject failure make much of the initial composition of its Cabinet.

- The historians J. N. Westwood and Ian Thatcher have claimed that the Provisional Government was initially 'popularly accepted'. Its members were, in the main, liberal-minded and some, such as Milyukov and Guchkov, were well-known political figures.
- Of more significance is the fact that the new government lacked legitimacy as it was an unelected body made up of members of the progressive bloc within the *Duma*.

Some historians have argued that the era of the Provisional Government was the only time that the Russian Empire was united. Others have pointed out that it was unlikely that the new government would have been able to sustain unity. It faced the following challenges from opponents:

- From the outset, authority was shared with the Petrograd Soviet, who opposed most of the Provisional Government's proposals and who had a good degree of popular support from workers, peasants, soldiers and sailors.
- The two groups disagreed over Russia's involvement in the war. The Provisional Government wanted to push on for 'a decisive victory' while the Petrograd Soviet demanded 'peace without annexations or indemnities' and also 'revolutionary defencism'.

- The war had captured the imagination of the populace; although some called for peace, this would have to be seen as honourable. This placed the government under much pressure to continue the war effort.
- The first version of the government (that is, the government that preceded the coalition with the Petrograd Soviet in May 1917) established a set of eight principles by which it would rule. These were classically liberal and included decrees on political amnesty and full freedom of speech. However, this allowed the proliferation of protest groups such as the Bolsheviks.
- The peasant land issue dragged on – due to the nature of the problem, the Provisional Government argued that only an elected assembly could deal with it. This irritated peasant groups who wanted more immediate action to be taken.

The historian Ian Thatcher has suggested that the opposition of General Kornilov to the government after July 1917 was the turning point in its fortunes. Thatcher has argued that the **Kornilov affair** was significant for a number of reasons.

- The Bolsheviks were viewed as heroes for organising the protection of Petrograd against Kornilov. They (the Soviet) were also 'armed' by the Provisional Government, a recipe for disaster.
- It was evident that the Provisional Government was susceptible to being challenged by the military and therefore others who might want to use force to seize power.
- The Kornilov affair showed Kerensky to be a weak leader compared with Lenin.
- Afterwards the Bolsheviks quickly gained more support so that by early September they had majorities in both the Petrograd and Moscow Soviets. By the end of October they had ousted the Provisional Government and taken control of Petrograd.

Overall, the Provisional Government struggled to deal with its opponents, but this was partly due to circumstance and not simply its incompetence.

Read the following interpretation and the two alternative answers to the question.

Which answer focuses more on the content and which one focuses more on the arguments of the interpretation? Explain your choice.

> Using your understanding of the historical context, assess how convincing the arguments in this passage are in relation to the start made by the Provisional Government in dealing with the challenges it faced.

The Provisional Government is often said to have got off to a weak start as it lacked legitimacy. In other words, it was appointed from a pool of people who had made up the progressive bloc in the old *Duma*; it was a government that had not been elected. Thatcher's argument is compelling in that it suggests the legitimacy argument is misleading. By stressing that the Provisional Government, even if it could have been considered legitimate, lacked authority and the will to exercise any power it might have had, Thatcher emphasises the precarious position the government was in from the start. Furthermore, the point that the so-called liberal reforms the Provisional Government carried out simply created havoc with respect to the administrative system makes sense when consideration is given to its 'eight principles' plan. The argument is supported by reference to the memoirs of a key political figure of the time; such records are not always considered by historians, although the passage gives little indication that they have been used critically. The passage ends by stressing how the Soviet was able to exploit the administrative chaos the Provisional Government created 'from the outset'; this is supported by the fact that Soviet Order Number 1 was issued in March 1917 and immediately put the Provisional Government on the back foot.

The passage is useful as it states that the Provisional Government lacked legitimacy but also authority. This is supported by memoirs of people who were there at the time, especially the liberal writer Nabokov. The founding member of the Kadet party believed that the Provisional Government created chaos in the administration of Russia as it carried out reforms that left it without any authority. This resulted in the Soviet gaining increasing influence over the government; it was, as Savich said at the time, the only body that indicated a forceful approach was needed to govern Russia successfully.

INTERPRETATION

Adapted from Ian D. Thatcher, Memoirs of the Russian Provisional Government in Revolutionary Russia *(2014), pages 3–4.*

The first steps made by the Provisional Government

Following the Tsar's abdication there could of course be any number of institutions that could claim power, just as at one time there had been several pretenders to the throne. The key question was authority. Legitimacy without authority is hollow. The memoirs of the leading Russian liberal, V.D. Nabokov, have been influential in the 'pessimist' view of the Provisional Government's (PG's) lack of authority. Nabokov was astounded by the PG's naivety in administration. One of its first acts was to abolish the governors and deputy governors. The dismantling of the old state also led to the loss of a functioning police force, the cessation of the State Council, and the mass dismissal of civilian and military personnel. It is little wonder that one of the main problems besetting the PG was that of its authority or the availability of some armed defence. For the Octobrist N.V. Savich, real authority lay with the Soviet of Workers' Deputies from the outset.

Key debate 2: Why is the Provisional Government often viewed as reluctant to carry out reforms?

REVISED

The Provisional Government paid little, if any, attention to economic and social reform. Its main aim was to enable reform of the political system through the setting up of a Constituent Assembly. By the start of January 1918 this had been achieved.

Despite the fact that the Provisional Government achieved its main aim, historians, such as Martin McCauley, have claimed that it could have carried out economic and social reforms that would have helped it maintain power. This would then have given the temporary regime the chance to prepare more thoroughly for elections to the new assembly. McCauley claims that 'the greatest feature of the government was inactivity'. His view is that the Provisional Government attempted the following but this was not enough to appease workers and peasants.

- Political prisoners were released.
- Secret courts were ended.
- Freedom of the press was instigated.

Furthermore, some historians have focused on how unwilling the Provisional Government was to make appropriate changes to deal with the challenges that gathered momentum after it came to power. In particular:

- There was a 'weak' attempt to unite the Provisional Government and Petrograd Soviet (May 1917) via a coalition government. Prince Lvov invited six members of the Petrograd Soviet to join, but elections to a Constituent Assembly, the ultimate political reform, were postponed.
- Land distribution issues, the main concern of peasants, were not addressed.
- Workers' committees were clamped down on, which seemed to contradict the liberal stance taken by the new government.
- Involvement in the war continued.

The lack of willingness and ability to deal with such challenges is said to have increased opposition, as shown by the **July Days**.

The major issues of worker demands for an eight-hour day and peasant demands for more land were largely ignored. Also, the government's policy of continuation of the war resulted in food shortages, inflation and demonstrations by workers, soldiers and sailors. By not being more reforming, the Provisional Government is considered to have incurred rejection by 'the vast majority of the army and population'. Hence, by the time the Constituent Assembly was put in place there was much grassroots scepticism about whether it would succeed.

The counter-argument to this is that the early changes made by the Provisional Government were not intended as reforms but as principles which would aid major political change. The lack of an economic and social programme of reform was understandable given the war situation, which had been inherited from the previous regime. McCauley's claim that there was a lack of urgency about the government seems unfair given the scope of internal and external challenges it faced (see page 86).

! Using knowledge to support or contradict

Below is a passage to read. Summarise the interpretation about the effectiveness of the Provisional Government's reforms and then develop a counter-argument.

Interpretation offered by the source:

_____

_____

Counter-argument:

_____

_____

_____

_____

PASSAGE A

Adapted from Mike Wells, Russia and its Rulers 1855–1964 _(2008), page 22._

The Provisional Government's approach to reform

The liberal reforms after March 1917 were more whole-hearted than those of the Tsars but freedom of press, movement, association, political activity and the end of political police and control added to the problem. The enemies of democracy got free rein. The ability to change enough to meet a crisis situation was a common feature of the Provisional Government and the Tsars. The peasant land seizures were neither prevented nor recognised, leaving a state of uncertainty in the countryside. If the government had issued a Land Decree accepting the new ownership, then perhaps the history of Russia might have been different. But that would have been asking the liberal middle class politicians to betray their entire ethos of respect for property and law and order.

! How far do you agree?

Read the following passage, then summarise each of its arguments. Use your knowledge to agree or contradict.

Argument in extract	Knowledge that corroborates	Knowledge that contradicts
1.		
2.		
3.		

PASSAGE B

Adapted from Orlando Figes, The February Revolution 1917 _(Section 5, www.orlandofiges.info)._

The aims of the Provisional Government and the immediate impact of its reforms

The Provisional Government saw itself as a wartime government of national confidence and salvation, above class or party interests, whose purpose was to see the country through to the ending of the war and the election of a Constituent Assembly, which alone could give a legal sanction to social and political reforms. With speed the Provisional Government passed a series of reforms in the spring of 1917. Russia overnight was effectively transformed into the 'freest country in the world' (Lenin). These reforms established a new culture of democracy. But the abstract language of political democracy was soon absorbed into ideas of social class. The word 'democracy' was popularly used as a social category: it was understood to mean the 'common people' or the 'labouring masses' whose opposite was not 'dictatorship' but the 'bourgeoisie'.

Key debate 3: How far was the First World War responsible for the fall of the Provisional Government?

The debate over the impact of the First World War on the Provisional Government can be engaged in by considering the so-called 'optimist' and 'pessimist' perspectives.

For the optimists, the formation of the Provisional Government was not a disaster and it was not necessarily doomed to fail – it was the continuation of the war that meant the new regime struggled to establish its authority. If Russia had pulled out of the war in March 1917, then maybe the Provisional Government would have succeeded, with the added possibility of the reinstatement of the tsar to create a constitutional monarchy.

More specifically, the optimists claim that the war hindered the progress of the Provisional Government as:

- The war had popular support – demands for withdrawal and peace were made on the basis that this would be honourable and unconditional. It was unlikely Germany would agree to such a deal, given its strong military position by March 1917.
- The war was costly in terms of the impact on land, labour (especially soldiers) and capital. The Provisional Government also felt committed to continuing the war, given that much had already been invested in trying to win it.
- The Provisional Government had limited support from its allies, Britain and France.
- Challenges such as land distribution and the impact on public health as a result of urbanisation were ignored – continuing with the war became a priority.

When these pressures related to the war are taken into consideration it is not surprising that the Provisional Government struggled to maintain authority. It does seem that the government was unlucky in that it was formed late in the war, when much of the damage to the economy and military had already occurred. In this respect, the optimists' view seems to hold some weight. However, critics of this perspective have argued that the Provisional Government was doomed to failure regardless of the war.

The pessimists believe that:

- The peoples of the Russian Empire viewed the Provisional Government as simply a variation on the tsarist regime. In fact, the Empire was in danger of disintegrating before the First World War; the new government struggled to contain demands for autonomy from Finland, Poland and the Ukraine (all major agricultural areas).
- Workers had already organised and campaigned for economic and social change before the war. By 1917, the soviets were in such a strong position that the Provisional Government was compelled to join with them to create a Dual Authority. This is evidence that the groundswell of popular protest had gained momentum over at least a decade and it was only a matter of time before the proletariat took control of the governance of Russia.
- Kerensky's leadership was suspect, especially when it came to dealing with opposition from Kornilov. He was not trusted by the workers and peasants, even though he had a socialist background.

The pessimist view is convincing to an extent – it stresses the need to see the revolution of 1917 as an event resulting from a multitude of pressures that built up over a long period of time and there is much evidence to support this. However, it downplays the impact of the First World War by suggesting it affected Russia in a similar way to previous wars. This neglects the point that the war was the first global, total war and, by definition, would have had a much greater effect than any military conflict witnessed before.

! Interpretations: content or argument? ⓐ

Read the following interpretation and the two alternative answers to the question.

Which answer focuses more on the content and which one focuses more on the arguments of the interpretation? Explain your choice.

> Using your understanding of the historical context, assess how convincing the arguments in this passage are about the impact of the First World War on the Provisional Government.

The interpretation states that the Provisional Government did not want to take Russia out of the First World War and even if it did, it lacked the ability to do so. Even though the government refined its approach by co-operating with the Soviet over the war effort, it failed to place Russia on a strong war footing. When Kerensky's military offensive of June 1917 failed, the population became increasingly disappointed with the Provisional Government; a prolonged period of social unrest emerged, known as the July Days. The interpretation then rightly goes on to show how the Provisional Government's preoccupation with the war meant that other issues, such as land distribution, were left by the wayside.

The interpretation is persuasive in that the war undoubtedly had an impact on how well the Provisional Government was able to function. The point that the government was unwilling and unable to take Russia out of the war is easily supported by the fact that, despite pressure from below, it was not until after the Bolsheviks seized power that an amnesty was agreed on (the Treaty of Brest-Litovsk). However, the argument put forward would appear to have at least two weaknesses. Firstly, it fails to highlight that Russia's war position had been inherited by the Provisional Government; the poor performance of the Russian military was mostly due to the failings of the tsar, Nicholas II. Secondly, the interpretation fails to highlight the growing strength of the Soviet and, by October, the rise in prominence of the Bolsheviks. The impact of the war is probably exaggerated, with the thrust of the argument focusing on the weaknesses of the Provisional Government rather than the strengths of its opposition.

INTERPRETATION

Adapted from Siobhan Peeling, Provisional Government, *1914–1918 online (2014).*

The Provisional Government: war, land and legitimacy

Many of the difficulties faced by the Provisional Government stemmed from its inability or reluctance to bring the war to an end. In the first cabinet, Foreign Minister Miliukov advocated the vigorous prosecution of the war to a decisive victory. When angry demonstrations over Miliukov's position brought about the downfall of the first coalition government, it adopted the Soviet's line of 'Revolutionary Defencism'. The war effort not only alienated the government from war-weary elements of the population and army: it also continued to strain state resources, disrupt food and fuel supplies, and limit the scope of domestic social and economic reform. Reforms addressing land hunger and a fair redistribution of the land to those who worked it were the priority for much of the peasantry, who made up the majority of the population. The Provisional Government, with its respect for legal rights and consciousness of the difficulty of carrying out land reform with millions of peasants in uniform at the front, deferred passing a land law. The authority of the government, which had always stressed its temporary mandate, crumbled. Peasants and deserting soldiers took land seizure into their own hands.

Key debate 4: To what extent did opposition from national minorities lead to the fall of the Provisional Government?

Opposition towards the Provisional Government from national minorities is a factor that is often overlooked when analysing the reasons for its demise. This is mainly due to the emphasis placed on the impact of the First World War and other problems inherited by the Provisional Government. One line of thought on this matter is that as the Provisional Government's main aim was to maintain the cohesiveness of the state until a Constituent Assembly could be instigated, it should have been a priority to assert authority across the whole of the Empire. Instead, the Provisional Government focused mainly on urban political, economic and social issues especially in Petrograd and Moscow. Some historians have stressed this was a mistake, as minorities:

- became frustrated that their wants and needs were not being addressed – the Provisional Government's slowness in creating an Assembly in which the minorities could express their views caused resentment and calls for autonomy
- were spurred on by the successes of workers, soldiers and sailors in establishing committees to demand more rights from employers and the government
- took advantage of the 'principles' adopted by the Provisional Government on which administration of the state was to be based (particularly the abolition of police units and provincial governors).

As a result, certain national minorities started to organise their own forms of provincial government, thus creating the possibility of the disintegration of the Empire.

- A Central *Rada* (council) was formed in Kiev in the Ukraine; its main aim was to press for the Ukraine to have autonomy.
- Similarly, in Finland, politicians campaigned for the establishment of their own *Sejm* (parliament) free from the influence of central Russian government.

It has been pointed out that such moves were not ignored by the Provisional Government. For example, demands for self-rule in the Transcaucasus were met with the formation of a Special Transcaucasian Committee. The problem with such initiatives, though, as in other regions such as Estonia and Latvia, was that they were often undermined by the formation of local soviets. This is evidence to show how more general issues of autonomy for regions was tied up with the more particular concerns of workers and peasants. When bodies such as the *Rada* and *Sejm* stated they would deal with local social and economic problems such as land distribution, they became 'a tier of unofficial opposition to policies announced in Petrograd'.

On the one hand, it seems reasonable to emphasise that the fortunes of the Provisional Government rested on how well they dealt with the challenges of a lack of legitimacy, the land question, urban unrest and the First World War. However, it also seems important to consider the strength of opposition from national minorities to the government and how the latter seemed to underestimate the strength of feeling at regional level. Given that, for example in Georgia, Estonia and the Ukraine, the majority of the population were peasants, it seems naïve for the Provisional Government not to have prioritised dealing with the land transference issue. Not getting a grip on the rise of nationalism in the regions of the Empire undoubtedly caused the Provisional Government further problems, as it enabled more left-wing parties to gain support at a local level.

ⓘ Using knowledge to support or contradict

Below is a passage to read. Summarise the interpretation about why the Provisional Government was faced with challenges from national minorities, then develop a counter-argument.

Interpretation offered by the source:

_____

_____

Counter-argument:

_____

_____

_____

_____

PASSAGE A

Adapted from Borislav Chernov, Shifts and Tensions in Ethnic/National Groups, _1914–1918 online (2014)._

The emergence of independent nation-states in the Russian Empire, February 1917–November 1917

The February Revolution in Russia marked the beginning of an extended period of imperial collapse in Central and Eastern Europe and the Middle East. Although the primary cause of the revolution was political – it reflected the inability of the imperial Russian establishment to inspire the confidence of the educated elites and the military – it was also linked to inter-ethnic relations. With the imperial centre gone irretrievably, national groups began to assert themselves and make bids for independence, as the weak Provisional Government in Petrograd looked on helplessly.

ⓘ How far do you agree?

Read the following passage, then summarise each of its arguments. Use your knowledge to agree or contradict.

Argument in extract	Knowledge that corroborates	Knowledge that contradicts
1.		
2.		
3.		

PASSAGE B

Adapted from Christopher Read, Revolutions and the Russian Empire, _1914–1918 online (2014)._

From February to the October Revolution, 1917

The period of less than eight months (February to the October Revolution) can be characterised as one in which a complex, widening set of interacting revolutions emerged and developed. The main driving force was a popular movement comprising peasants, workers, soldiers, and sailors who began to assert their rights and demands through a vast network of for the most part spontaneously organised committees. The overwhelming majority of the population was associated with this movement in one form or another. However, the situation was further complicated, not least by the fundamental divisions within the elites; the right demanded 'order' through firm authoritarianism and, if necessary, a military dictatorship. Liberals sought to establish a form of representative democracy. In addition, there was an increasing number of national revolutions, with Finns, Poles and, more ambiguously, Ukrainians in the forefront. Add to this the crucial social revolutions, with gender revolution as an important component, as well as cultural and religious revolution and the period takes on a massive complexity. It has been rightly called a 'kaleidoscope of revolutions'.

Exam focus

Below is an exam-style depth-study question on the Provisional Government and a model answer. Read it and the comments around it.

Evaluate the interpretations in both of the two passages and explain which you think is more convincing as an explanation of the failures of the Provisional Government.

PASSAGE A

Adapted from J. N. Westwood, Endurance and Endeavour: Russian History 1812–2001, *page 224.*

With successive reshuffles that gave moderate socialists more influence, the Provisional Government lasted more than seven months. This in itself was quite an achievement, for it had little power and faced enormous problems. The Soviet's Order No. 1 threatened to deprive the government of an effective army. The old police, by general consent, had been disbanded, but the militia which was to replace them never became an effective force. The Soviet, because it controlled the workers' organisations, could deny vital services if it so chose; thus the measures taken by the Provisional Government needed the acquiescence of the Soviet leaders if they were to be effective. The Provisional Government, co-opted from the members of a Duma elected on a narrow franchise and consisting of gentlemen favouring a western-style parliamentary democracy, could hardly claim to be a popular government, even though it was popularly accepted for the time being.

PASSAGE B

Adapted from Peter Oxley, Russia: 1855–1919 From Tsars to Commissars, *page 91.*

After the Romanov dynasty collapsed there was, in the words of the historian Christopher Read, 'a nationwide honeymoon. For the only time in its history, the Russian Empire was united'. The new Provisional Government had to face those same problems, exacerbated by Russia's involvement in the war, that the tsarist government had failed to solve, as well as to meet the eager expectations of 160 million people. In fact the Provisional Government proved quite unable to deliver what was expected. It was increasingly seen as a product of the old regime and as unrepresentative of the Russian people. Perhaps it would have been impossible for any government to succeed in the circumstances it inherited. The government lasted only a few weeks before being replaced by another, and then another. The 'honeymoon' was soon over and its authority gradually slipped away.'

The two passages have much in common. They both stress that the make-up of the Provisional Government (PG) and the challenges it faced made it difficult for it to get off to a good start. Although there is some acknowledgement of a degree of success for the government, both Passage A and Passage B make nothing of the fact that the Constituent Assembly was instituted in a relatively short period of time. Passage A is quite convincing as an interpretation about why the PG struggled. There is much evidence to support the argument that the strength of the Petrograd Soviet made it almost impossible for the PG to achieve anything that did not meet the approval of workers. Although Passage B is quite persuasive in arguing that the context made it difficult for the government to succeed, it gives little credit to the strength of leadership and administration of workers' organisations.

A sound observation is made in the introduction about how both passages stress the challenges faced by the Provisional Government. There is also comment about how both show similarity in omission of a key development (the establishment of the Constituent Assembly).

Passage A highlights the weak position the PG found itself in due to having limited authority especially when matched against the Soviet. However, the validity of this observation can be challenged by the fact that the eight principles upon which the new government based its reforms would inevitably have led to a reduction in its authority. In other words, the lack of power of the PG was down its own making. At least Westwood highlights the relative strength of the Soviet, which is often downplayed by historians who believe that the Romanov dynasty was resilient and could deal with opposition from workers but could not cope with the challenges thrown up by the First World War. Passage A makes much of the fact that the PG was the product of the 'old regime' and therefore that it was unlikely to be popular from the start. Recent research, however, suggests that the PG was initially welcomed simply because it was a new departure and promised hope for the future. Also, Passage A does not touch on the war issue even when highlighting the strengths of the Soviet. This is a serious omission as throughout its period of tenure the PG struggled to deal with the military, political, economic and social challenges thrown up by the conflict.

> The response highlights that A stresses the strength of workers' organisations (the soviets); much recent research supports this view. Also, the analysis contains comment on the lack of mention of the impact of the First World War and rightly highlights this as a 'serious omission'.

Passage B fails to provide any discussion of the role of the Soviet. Oxley does, though, offer some explanation of why the PG went for a liberal approach to governing where he states that it had to 'meet the eager expectations of 160 million people.' The people, influenced by the Soviet, expected progress to be made with respect to social and economic issues and personal freedoms. On the issue of legitimacy, Passage B, implies that the Russian people welcomed the PG as it was believed that it signified a new and brighter future. While it is true that the make-up of the PG consisted of members of the old *Duma*, this did not necessarily mean it would be rejected out of hand. In fact, the PG contained many unfamiliar characters and the general populace would probably not have recognised their names. In this sense, and given the eight principles for reform, the PG is likely to have had more grassroots support, at least at the start. Finally, only Passage B mentions the all-important issue of the First World War. Many of the challenges faced by the PG stemmed from the war. In particular, the issue of withdrawing from the conflict was not dealt with satisfactorily by the PG. It was forced into compromising over this with the Soviet by accepting the latter's demand for 'revolutionary defencism' and a negotiated peace with no annexations or indemnities. This strengthens the case for B being a more convincing account.

Overall, Passage B is the more balanced and accurate interpretation of the failure of the PG, although it does lack some support and development. Passage A makes some salient points but perhaps focuses too strongly on the role of the Soviet and does not consider the challenges faced by the PG associated with the war. Current research on this topic emphasises how any type of government installed in Russia in March 1917 would have struggled to meet the war-related challenges it faced.

> This is a very solid and well-considered conclusion. A clear judgement is reached that is very much in line with the answer as a whole.

The answer is very well focused on the question. There is clear awareness of the wider debate over the performance of the Provisional Government. A reasonable depth of contextual knowledge is deployed to evaluate the interpretations and reach a judgement. The answer is worthy of a mark in the higher levels of the mark scheme.

Moving towards Level 6

Use the comments and the mark scheme in order to move the response to the very top of Level 6, making a list of the additional features that would enable the answer to achieve full marks. Remember it does not have to be a perfect answer, but one that best fits with the descriptors.

Key debate 1: How far did de-Stalinisation represent a genuine break from the past?

REVISED

From the 1920s until Khrushchev became Prime Minister in 1958, Russian communists, on the whole, believed that the Communist Party existed to develop ideology and to oversee the government. Quite simply, the role of the Soviet government was to supervise the running of Russia. Under Stalin, the Party and government lost any freedoms they had and were answerable directly to him. The government became an organ which put into operation Stalin's policies.

Khrushchev wanted to move away from the highly centralised and personalised mode of government established by Stalin. To do this, he created a government that was more accountable to him but also to the Party.

However, the historian Martin McCauley has proposed that Khrushchev only 'changed aspects of the [political] system and not the system itself.' Thus, he is seen to have been successful in:

- making the Communist Party more accountable to the people
- reforming bureaucracy so it appeared less corrupt and more effective in dealing with the wants and needs of the population.

But McCauley believes that tinkering with the system and redirecting power to the Party had a limited impact on presenting Russia, to the rest of the world, as a country that was moving away from the Stalinist years. This is mainly seen as a result of Khrushchev's adherence to the centralised planning of the economy and reluctance to embrace an economic system at least partly based on market forces. His critics seemed to detect a contradiction between his political and economic policies.

McCauley's interpretation seems rather harsh given the context Khrushchev was working in and the underlying assumption made about the value of a more market-based economy. The Stalinist regime had built up a great deal of mistrust in the West about Soviet intentions during the early years of the Cold War. Through de-Stalinisation Khrushchev could be viewed as having done his best to make relations with the West more cordial. Also, it is debatable whether a market-based or capitalist economy was and is the right way for any country to improve living standards.

Khrushchev experienced a degree of opposition from peasants and workers. Some have argued that during the Khrushchev era, there was very little rural unrest. J. N. Westwood has pointed out that 'for the first time since Peter the Great there was a genuine interchange between the tsar and people'. This was due to the fact that Khrushchev 'spent much of his time in the countryside, conferring with party secretaries, cajoling farm chairmen, and making promises to peasants in the kind of earthy language they could understand'. Despite this, Khrushchev's agricultural policies, especially the Virgin Lands campaign, were not especially appealing to the Russian people; they soon started to express their discontent. When this happened Khrushchev was not afraid to resort to force to deal with the unrest.

Another area of debate over opposition to Khrushchev concerns his eventual downfall. This is commonly attributed to:

- the failure of Khrushchev's agricultural policy
- loss of prestige over the Cuban Missile Crisis
- deterioration in relations with China
- Khrushchev's decentralisation of the government, which appeared to threaten the positions of key members of the bureaucracy
- defence cuts, which annoyed the military.

The historian Norman Lowe has suggested that this is a rather simplistic way of looking at why the Russian leader was eventually 'persuaded' to step down. He believes the reasons were of a more personal nature:

'Perhaps his colleagues were tired of his extrovert personality (once, in a heated moment at the United Nations, he took off his shoe and hammered the table with it) and felt he was taking too much on himself. Khrushchev had become increasingly aggressive and arrogant, and at times seemed to have developed the "cult of personality" almost as much as Stalin.'

However, some historians such as Dmitri Volkogonov, a critic of all Soviet leaders, believe that Khrushchev, through de-Stalinisation, 'achieved virtually the impossible' as 'in a fundamental way [he] also changed society.' It was probably these core changes made by Khrushchev that worried his contemporaries the most. It is likely that they viewed them as a predecessor to even more radical reforms and the deconstruction of the communist system in Russia.

Summarise the arguments

Below is a sample exam question and one of the passages referred to in the question.

You must read the passage and identify the interpretation offered. Look for the arguments of the passage.

> With reference to the passage and your contextual knowledge, how convincing do you find the passage as an explanation for Khrushchev's motives for introducing de-Stalinisation?

Interpretation offered by the source:

_____

_____

PASSAGE

From Richard Cavendish, Nikita Khrushchev: his famous speech on 'The Personality Cult and its Consequences' (February 25th, 1956) (History Today, *Volume 56, Issue 2, February 2006*).

Nikita Khrushchev and his 'Secret Speech'

The twentieth congress of the Communist Party of the Soviet Union assembled in Moscow in the Great Hall of the Kremlin on February 14th, 1956. It was the first since the death of Josef Stalin in 1953, but almost nothing was said about the dead leader until, in closed session on the 25th, 1,500 delegates and many invited visitors listened to an amazing speech by Nikita Khrushchev, First Secretary of the party, on 'The Personality Cult and its Consequences'. Khrushchev denounced Stalin, the cult of personality he had fostered and the crimes he had perpetrated, including the execution, torture and imprisonment of loyal party members on false charges. He blamed Stalin for foreign policy errors, for the failings of Soviet agriculture, for ordering mass terror and for mistakes that had led to appalling loss of life in the Second World War and the German occupation of huge areas of Soviet territory. Khrushchev's audience heard him in almost complete silence, broken only by astonished murmurs. The delegates did not dare even to look at each other as the party secretary piled one horrifying accusation on another for four solid hours. At the end there was no applause and the audience left in a state of shock. It was an extraordinarily dangerous and daring thing for Khrushchev to do. Solzhenitsyn believed that he spoke out of 'a movement of the heart', a genuine impulse to do good. Others have pointed out, more cynically, that it tarred other party leaders with the Stalinist brush, to the ostentatiously repentant Khrushchev's advantage. It deflected blame from the party and the system on to Stalin's shoulders. A few months later it was announced that the congress had called for measures 'for removing wholly and entirely the cult of the individual, foreign to Marxism-Leninism ... in every aspect of party, governmental and ideological activity.'

Key debate 2: To what extent were the economic and social reforms made by Khrushchev a failure?

A fairly common view is that Khrushchev attempted to make some quite innovative and radical changes but was largely unsuccessful due to a lack of co-operation from senior Communist Party officials and bureaucrats. Some historians though, such as Donald Filtzer, have suggested that Khrushchev's schemes were poorly thought out; it was this that caused a change in the initial level of support he had for his ideas.

Filtzer has argued that Khrushchev's reforms were often seen as 'hare-brained' [poorly thought out] for the following reasons:
- Reforms such as the Virgin Lands programme were well intended but were badly planned – initially, grain production increased substantially but this tailed off due to the poor quality of land used and a lack of fertilisers.
- The highly bureaucratic Soviet 'system' was too cumbersome to allow for reforms to be implemented quickly enough.
- Khrushchev failed to realise that some Communist Party members may have felt threatened by the changes he made.
- The reforms were not as radical as they needed to be to cope with the challenges left by the Stalinist regime (such as the 'backwardness' of industry and agriculture).

This view has been challenged by historians such as Norman Lowe, who have emphasised that Khrushchev's reforms were a considerable achievement given the context in which he was working. Stalin had left agriculture in a perilous state and Russian industry had mainly been geared up to meet the demands of war (the Second World War and the Cold War). Khrushchev recognised this and did his best to address these problems. Thus, Lowe has argued that:
- It was only in 1963 that a significant fall in grain production was witnessed and that was mainly down to poor weather; the weaknesses of the Virgin Lands scheme have therefore probably been exaggerated.
- Khrushchev made quite a radical change to the industrial infrastructure (in a relatively short period) by focusing on the establishment of light industries (those that produced consumer products. This seemed to raise living standards – for example, from 1955 to 1966, the number of washing machines per thousand of the population increased from one to 77.
- The Russian leader had to prioritise, to an extent, political problems. Furthermore, such problems were dealt with effectively through, for example, the ending of Stalinist Gulags and the placing of the NKVD under the control of the Party and the state.

Therefore, McCauley's view that Khrushchev's reforms made him a 'courageous failure' seems rather simplistic. Given the challenges he faced, Khrushchev did much to improve the lives of Russian peoples in a short period of time.

! Using knowledge to support or contradict

Below is an extract to read. You are asked to summarise the interpretation about the outcome of Khrushchev's Virgin Lands campaign and then develop a counter-argument.

Interpretation offered by the source:

_____

_____

Counter-argument:

_____

_____

EXTRACT

Adapted from Orlando Figes, Khrushchev's Virgin Lands Campaign *(2014).*

Khrushchev's Virgin Lands campaign

The most ambitious of Khrushchev's reforms was the Virgin Lands campaign, in which hundreds of thousands of young men and women volunteered to work and settle on the steppelands of Kazakhstan. Khrushchev promoted the campaign as a 'Leninist' response to the crisis of collectivised agriculture. The collective farms were too inefficient to feed the Soviet population. Propaganda trumpeted the achievements of the settlers on the Virgin Lands. But its results were mixed: 40 million hectares of new land were brought into production between 1954 and 1963, and grain output rose as a result, enough to end food shortages in the short term; but harvest yields were variable, and steadily declined from 1958, largely because there was not enough fertilizer to compensate for the poor soil.

How far do you agree?

Read the following passage, then summarise each of its arguments. Use your knowledge to agree or contradict.

Argument in extract	Knowledge that corroborates	Knowledge that contradicts
1.		
2.		
3.		

PASSAGE

Adapted from Melanie Ilic, Soviet State and Society under Nikita Khrushchev *(2009), pages 1–3.*

Khrushchev and the 'thaw'

Historians have come to term the decade or so following the death of Stalin in 1953 as the 'thaw'; the word is used as a metaphor not only for the early signs of relaxation in the international Cold War tensions, but also for the easing of the frosty cultural and social relations that existed within the Soviet Union. After 1956, Khrushchev's promotion of 'peaceful coexistence with the West' included the belief that the Soviet Union should imitate and borrow from capitalist countries in order to boost the socialist economy. His aim was that the Soviet Union should eventually overtake the capitalist economies in levels of output and growth. To some extent, Khrushchev's aims to modernise the Soviet Union, to bring the country prosperity and success, to improve health and welfare and to raise the everyday living standards of the Soviet population can be seen as common goals of all contemporary governments. His period of office notably saw the emergence of a material culture and the beginnings of a consumer society in the Soviet Union.

Key debate 3: How effectively did Khrushchev deal with the challenges posed by the Cold War?

When Khrushchev became the leader of Russia, the Cold War was already under way. He faced the challenge of dealing with the aftermath of the Korean War, dissent in Eastern Europe against Russian influence and managing a nuclear arms race. How well he dealt with these three issues has been debated extensively by historians.

One perspective, especially at the time, is that Khrushchev was seen to have a number of successes:

- The death of Stalin and the end of the Korean War (July 1953) and Indo-China War (1954) seemed to influence Russian leaders to alter their stance on the Cold War. In Khrushchev's 'Secret Speech' of February 1956 he stated that for Russian foreign policy: 'There are only two ways – either peaceful co-existence [with the West] or the most destructive war in history. There is no third way.' The change of policy can be viewed as a success as the Russian leader was seen to be taking the initiative in attempting to create a more peaceful and secure world.
- Khrushchev supported the signing of the Austrian State Treaty (May 1955). This indicated that Russia was willing to co-operate with the West over dealing with Austria's claims for independence.
- The thaw in the Cold War, epitomised by the policy of 'peaceful co-existence', prompted Russia's satellite states to demand more freedom. When this appeared to get out of control, as in the case of Hungary in 1956, Khrushchev, using Russian tanks, was quick to react. The Budapest rising was ruthlessly suppressed, which gained Khrushchev support from the Communist Party in Russia.
- In 1961, Khrushchev proposed to the American government that the West should come out of Berlin. This demand was prompted by the increasing number of East Germans trying to flee to the Western sector. President Kennedy refused to agree to the idea, causing Khrushchev to support the construction of the Berlin Wall. Again, back in Russia this was seen as a bold move to prevent further embarrassment to fellow communist leaders in East Germany.
- Khrushchev's handling of the Cuban Missile Crisis (1962) is sometimes praised as he initially tested Kennedy's diplomatic and decision skills before agreeing to a relaxation of tensions. Some historians have argued that Khrushchev forced Kennedy to compromise rather than call the Russian leader's bluff by invading Cuba and overthrowing Castro. Also, the compromise can be viewed as a Russian success as it resulted in the 'hot line' telephone link between Moscow and Washington. By agreeing on a more direct, quick way of solving disputes the hot line strengthened the Russian 'peaceful co-existence' stance.

Some critics of Khrushchev, though, have been quick to identify flaws in his approach to dealing with Cold War challenges.

For some, commenting at the time and since, Khrushchev's Cold War policy was too risky. Rather than creating stability, it is often viewed as leading to heightened tensions.

- Peaceful co-existence was viewed by some communists as a betrayal of ideals; it was perceived as a U-turn with respect to spreading communism internationally. In particular, the Chinese communists accused the Russian leader of being 'too soft on imperialists'; this criticism led to Khrushchev withdrawing military support when the Chinese needed it.
- The historian Martin McCauley has argued that the Hungarian crisis of 1956 was a 'disaster' that could be blamed on de-Stalinisation. Furthermore, he believes: 'it put back the cause of de-Stalinisation, and hence reform, in Eastern Europe and also weakened the Soviet cause abroad. Communist parties in western Europe lost many members and declined in influence.' The ruthless suppression of Hungarian protesters was viewed as a 'poor advertisement' for communism.
- The erection of the Berlin Wall can also be seen as an oppressive measure and one that worsened relations with the West.
- By taking Kennedy to the brink during the Cuban Missile Crisis, Khrushchev was seen as someone who nearly provoked what would have been a catastrophic nuclear war. Moreover, by agreeing to withdraw missiles from Cuba, the Russian leader was seen by fellow Russian officials as someone who had backed down. This is often cited as being a main factor in Khrushchev's demise.

The debate over Khrushchev's handling of the Cold War seems to hinge on whether he is seen as 'inspirational and innovative' (by trying to instil peaceful co-existence) or 'erratic and impulsive' (by not being consistent) or both.

Summarise the arguments

Below is a sample exam question and one of the extracts referred to in the question.

You must read the extract and identify the interpretation offered. Look for the arguments of the passage.

> With reference to the extract and your contextual knowledge, how convincing do you find the extract as an explanation of Khrushchev' success in handling the Berlin Crisis of 1958–62?

Interpretation offered by the source:

_____

_____

EXTRACT

Adapted from Vladislav M. Zubkov, Khrushchev and the Berlin Crisis: 1958–62 *(2003).*

Khrushchev and the Berlin Crisis

The Berlin Crisis was not a product of Khrushchev's bad temper. He started the Crisis because he was genuinely concerned by West German designs against the GDR and for nuclear armament. Even the threat of the 'loss' of the GDR was intolerable in those times for the Soviet leadership. Inspired in all likelihood by the crisis in the Far East, Khrushchev hoped to force the United States to acquiesce to the existence of 'two Germanys' just as they had acquiesced in, indeed supported the existence of, 'two Chinas' in the Far East. Khrushchev always expected to manage the Crisis without resorting to brinkmanship with the United States. In the first year of the Crisis his diplomacy scored an unexpected success: the trip to the United States and Eisenhower's acceptance of a return invitation to come to the Soviet Union. But during the second year, when the U-2 incident occurred and the prospect of détente faded, Khrushchev found himself a hostage of his political and ideological commitments. Instead of maintaining the tension to bring the West to the negotiating table, the Soviet leader tied his own hands by a promising to sign a separate peace treaty with the GDR. As Sino-Soviet relations deteriorated, many in the Kremlin, including Khrushchev himself, began to wonder if it would not be better to ally the Soviet foreign policy with a militant Chinese line rather than to continue to play diplomatic games with the West. The pressures from Ulbricht certainly contributed to this dilemma.

Key debate 4: 'Courageous failure' – how valid is this assessment of Khrushchev's policy towards minorities, satellite states and Asia?

Khrushchev has been viewed as a 'courageous failure' when it comes to his domestic and foreign policies. With respect to minorities, satellite states and Asia the 'courageous' label stems from de-Stalinisation and the policy of 'peaceful co-existence'. Critics of Khrushchev have highlighted the following failures of his 'courageous' policies:

- Khrushchev attempted to resolve conflict with Tito and Yugoslavia through appeasement. It is argued that by allowing Tito a certain amount of autonomy, other Eastern European states were encouraged to follow the Yugoslavian model. This created instability in the Soviet bloc and may even have contributed to the final collapse of communism in 1991.
- The Hungarian crisis of 1956 is said to have ended in disaster for two reasons. Firstly, it appeared that, by using force, Khrushchev had resorted to Stalinist tactics to deal with opposition. De-Stalinisation and, therefore, the prospect of further liberal reforms in Eastern Europe suffered a major setback. Secondly, communist parties in the West lost support, which dented the prospect of communism spreading outside of the Soviet Union.
- With respect to the German question, Khrushchev's approach resulted in the construction of the Berlin Wall. As with the Hungarian uprising, this suggested that Khrushchev was too willing to resort to repression when his more liberal policies failed.
- De-Stalinisation seemed to worsen relations with China as Khrushchev struggled to deal with the criticisms from his Chinese counterpart. According to the historian Martin McCauley, from as early as 1954, 'the wily Mao bamboozled Khrushchev', suggesting that the Soviet leader was no match for his Chinese counterpart. By the 1960s the Chinese were claiming that they, rather than Khrushchev's Soviet Union, were the real upholders of Marxism-Leninism. This caused communist parties throughout the communist world to start to take sides, which divided the movement, something that would not have been conceivable under Stalin.

Defenders of Khrushchev have argued that he was more of a 'courageous success' than a failure when it came to his dealings with minorities, satellite states and Asia. In particular, they believe that the following achievements are often sidelined:

- Khrushchev managed to gain support from Tito over the Hungarian uprising.
- He also got the backing of other socialist states (Poland, Czechoslovakia, Romania and Bulgaria) as well as China for his handling of the Hungarian crisis. Also, the West failed to intervene, which meant Khrushchev had scored something of a propaganda victory.
- The Soviet leader's stance on Germany prevented the West from taking total control of the country and its capital, Berlin.
- Mao's attempt to manipulate the Soviets failed. Khrushchev held his own against Mao and on more than one occasion showed China that he was prepared to take a strong position against them. For example, in 1958 the Soviet Union declined to provide China with military support in its conflict with Taiwan and the USA.

⚠ Using knowledge to support or contradict

Below is a passage to read. Summarise the interpretation about the causes of the Sino-Soviet split during Khrushchev's rule and then develop a counter-argument.

Interpretation offered by the source:

_____

_____

Counter-argument:

_____

_____

_____

_____

PASSAGE A

Adapted from Lorenz M. Lüthi, The Sino-Soviet Split: Cold War in the Communist World _(2008)._

The Sino-Soviet split during Khrushchev's rule

The Sino-Soviet split during Khrushchev's rule was mainly the result of disputes over Marxist-Leninist ideology. The first point of ideological disagreement between the Soviet Union and China emerged in 1955 over the Stalinist socioeconomic development model. Facing a structural economic crisis, Mao replaced the development model that the People's Republic of China (PRC) had inherited from the late Josef Stalin with a development strategy resembling earlier Soviet policies that had already been discredited in the Union of Socialist Soviet Republics (USSR). Despite its failure, Mao returned to their basic ideas in the Great Leap Forward of 1958–60, only to reap disaster. De-Stalinisation in the Soviet Union provided the second moment of ideological conflict. While Khrushchev's Secret Speech in February 1956 was rooted mainly in domestic necessities, it reverberated throughout the socialist world. As a result, over the course of 1956 and 1957, Mao and Khrushchev took up opposite positions on Stalin as a theoretician and practitioner. Third, Sino-Soviet ideological disputes arose over the correct method of dealing with imperialism. Launched in early 1956 as well, Khrushchev's policy of peaceful coexistence with the United States did not cause immediate conflict with the Chinese Communists because they were preoccupied with de-Stalinisation. From late 1957, however, tensions over this policy grew, and, by the mid-1960s, dominated Sino Soviet relations. Most other points of Sino-Soviet conflict were either the result of these ideological disagreements or of lesser importance. Security disputes – such as the Second Taiwan Strait Crisis in 1958 – and economic disagreements – in particular trade and the sudden withdrawal of the Soviet specialists from China in 1960 – arose as the consequence of ideological arguments.

⚡ How far do you agree?

Read the above passage, then summarise each of the arguments in the passage about the reasons for the Sino-Soviet split during the rule of Khrushchev. Use your knowledge to corroborate (agree with) or to challenge (disagree with) the arguments.

Argument in extract	Knowledge that corroborates	Knowledge that challenges
1.		
2.		
3.		

Exam focus

Read the question and Passages A and B below about the response of China to Russia's invasion of Hungary in 1956 and then the example conclusions (Responses A and B) that follow:

Evaluate the interpretations in both of the two passages and explain which you think is more convincing as an explanation of the importance of the response of the Chinese leader Mao to Russia's invasion of Hungary in 1956.

PASSAGE A

Adapted from Michael Lynch, Origins and development of authoritarian and single-party states *(2013), page 126.*

1956 was the year that the new Soviet leader, Nikita Khrushchev, shook the communist world by launching an extraordinary attack on his predecessor, Joseph Stalin, who had died three years earlier. Khrushchev denounced Stalin and his 'cult of personality'. Mao could see how easily this charge could be made against him in China. His apparent encouragement of criticism from within the Party, was, therefore, a way of taking the sting out of the suggestion and preventing the comparison being made between him and Stalin. However, if Mao had indeed launched the 100 Flowers Campaign [the Maoist policy, established by 1957, of allowing Chinese leadership to be discussed and criticised] out of fear of being compared with Stalin, the fear temporarily lessened in 1956. In November of that year Khrushchev sent Soviet tanks into Budapest to crush the Hungarian Uprising. That was the Soviet leader's way of making it clear that de-Stalinisation did not mean the lessening of the grip of the Communist Party over the USSR or the weakening of Soviet control over the Eastern bloc.

Mao fully approved of the Soviet action for two reasons. In the first place, he believed it was the kind of tough line that communist governments should take in order to maintain their authority. In the second, he was relieved by the knowledge that the Soviet Union had merely been flirting with liberal ideas. This meant that he did not need to compete with Khrushchev in the defence of hardline communism. Neither leader had any intention of relaxing his political control over the people.

PASSAGE B

Adapted from William Taubman, Khrushchev: the man and his era *(2003), pages 295–97.*

Early on 24 October thousands of Soviet troops and tanks entered Budapest. But instead of pacifying the city, they deepened the crisis. When armoured vehicles were surrounded by Molotov cocktail-wielding youths, Hungarian security forces offered little support, and some went over to the rebels. By midafternoon at least twenty-five protesters had been killed, and more than two hundred injured. By October 30 hundreds of Hungarian civilians and Soviet soldiers had died. The situation seemed more dire than ever yet the Presidium in Moscow decided to accept it. General Zhukov, for example, stated that "we should withdraw our troops from Budapest and from all of Hungary if that's demanded". Khrushchev seemed to agree with the idea of "a peaceful path, the withdrawal of troops and negotiations" although he was clearly uncomfortable with it. Apart from the possibility of losing Hungary Khrushchev agonised about rebellion spreading to its neighbours. Student demonstrations in Romania had led the Bucharest authorities to close their border with Hungary. Czechoslovakia and East Germany seemed vulnerable as well. The Soviet bloc threatened to crumble.

Beginning on 23 October Khrushchev had sought the advice of the Chinese. Initially, Mao urged that "the working class of Hungary should be allowed to regain control of the situation and put down the uprising on its own". But by 30 October, having heard about the lynching of a Hungarian secret policeman in Budapest, Mao changed his mind. That Khrushchev needed advice from Mao confirms his crisis of confidence. However, with or without Chinese sanction (the issue of when and how Khrushchev learned of Mao's change of position remains unclear), Khrushchev reversed his stance on 31 October. He told the Presidium "we must ... not pull troops out of the Budapest. We must take the initiative and restore order in Hungary. If we leave Hungary, that will encourage the Americans, English and French, the imperialists. They will perceive it as a weakness and go on the offensive".

Response A

In conclusion, Passage B offers a more convincing view of Mao's response to Khrushchev's decision to invade Hungary in 1956. The passage offers a balanced answer considering both Mao's view of the invasion and Khrushchev's response independent of the advice given by the Chinese leader. It is accurate in the details given about the timing, extent and immediate impact of the invasion. In particular, it highlights the possibility that unrest might escalate and spread throughout Eastern Europe which prompted the final responses of both Mao and Khrushchev. Passage A glosses over the details of the invasion (and is misleading about the timing of it) which are important in aiding understanding about the changing views held by the Chinese and Russian leaders.

Response B

Both passages correctly acknowledge that Mao's response to Khrushchev's actions over the Hungarian uprising was important in that it was supportive. However, they differ with respect to the motives and timing of Mao's response. Passage A implies Mao's response came after Khrushchev sent troops and tanks to Hungary whereas Passage B makes the important point that Khrushchev consulted Mao before making his decision. But Passage A is more explicit about Mao's reasoning; by the mid-1950s the Chinese leader was indeed concerned that his 'ally' was drifting from hardline communism. Passage B however, infers that Mao's interest in Hungary was based on his wish to preserve the freedoms of workers, which would have been in line with communist ideology. Finally, Passage A gives the impression that relations between China and Russia were fairly cordial and that they were following a similar path; they were both concerned to present the image that communist control over 'the people' would not be relaxed. This view ignores the fact that the two states were becoming increasingly antagonistic towards each other. Passage B hints at this by highlighting how Khrushchev was willing to consult Mao initially, but in the end made up his own mind as to how to respond to the Hungarian crisis. Therefore, overall, Passage B provides the more convincing explanation of the importance of Mao's response to Khrushchev's decision making.

Analysis of responses A and B

Both conclusions offer a judgement and both support their claims. However, Response B is the stronger conclusion:

- Response A focuses almost exclusively on Passage B, with mention of Passage A only towards the end.
- Response B compares the two Interpretations in reaching its judgement and is more balanced.
- Response B, although it argues that Passage B is stronger, does not dismiss the valid points made in Passage A.

Characteristics of strong Interpretation answers

You have now considered three sample high-level responses to Interpretations questions. Use these responses to make a bullet-pointed list of the characteristics of a strong interpretation answer. Use this list when planning and writing your own practice exam responses.

Glossary

1936 Constitution   Often referred to as Stalin's Constitution, this introduced significant political changes, including the introduction of universal suffrage. Separate nation states were also given greater representation in the centralised government of the USSR.

1905 Revolution   The 1905 Revolution consisted of a series of protests and strikes that led to the publication of the October Manifesto and the creation of the *Duma*.

Agitprop   The Agitation and Propaganda Department (Agitprop) was set up towards the end of the Civil War to maintain control over the dissemination of socialist ideas and encourage acceptance of the official socialist ideology.

Agro-towns   Towns focused on agricultural production, where the majority of inhabitants are agricultural workers.

Austria–Hungary   A dual monarchy ruled by the Habsburgs between 1867 and 1918.

Autarky   A policy of economic self-sufficiency.

Autocracy   A system of government in which one person has absolute authority. The Russian tsars believed this power was ordained by God.

Balkan Wars of 1912–1913   This term refers to two conflicts, the first of which began in 1912 when the Balkan League went to war with the Ottoman Empire. The conflict ended in May 1913 and resulted in significant territorial gains for the Balkan nations. However, a second conflict soon erupted between Bulgaria and Serbia. The latter was victorious, having gained the support of the other Balkan nations and also the Ottomans.

Berlin Blockade   In June 1948 the Western powers combined to introduce a new currency in the zones under their control. Russia saw this as an attempt to show how capitalism could bring prosperity to Berlin and retaliated by blocking all communication links with the western part of the city. The blockade was eventually lifted in May 1949.

Berlin Wall   A wall erected in 1961 in Berlin by the Russian authorities to formally separate the East from the West. The aim was to stop people escaping to the Western zones.

Bloody Sunday   In January 1905, 200 demonstrators marching on the Winter Palace were shot dead by soldiers and a further 800 were injured.

Bolsheviks   A breakaway group which formed when the Russian Social Democratic Labour Party splintered into two factions. The Bolsheviks were considered the majority group, whereas the other group, the Mensheviks, were considered the minority.

Bourgeoisie   The ruling class who possessed control over the means of production.

Capitalism   An economic system based on private ownership of the means of production and driven by the profit motive.

Cheka   The Russian Extraordinary Commission for the Struggle Against Counter Revolution and Sabotage, founded in late 1917.

Collectivisation   A system in which peasants shared resources to produce food which was then distributed to the local community. Surpluses were sent to urban populations.

Cominform   The Communist Information Bureau set up in 1947 to co-ordinate economic recovery for Eastern Europe.

Comintern   The Communist international body established in March 1918. Its aim was to spread Communism overseas.

Command economy   An economy controlled completely by the state.

Communist utopia   The idea that communism would lead to an ideal form of society.

Constituent Assembly   An assembly of politicians which would be elected by the people.

Cult of personality   A cult surrounding a particularly charismatic and enigmatic individual.

Dekulakisation   A policy aimed at abolishing what was perceived as a class of wealthy peasants.

De-Stalinisation   Khrushchev's denunciation of Stalin's policies.

Dictatorship   A system of government in which one person or group is invested with absolute authority, but not through God. The authority is often assumed after force is used to seize power.

Dictatorship of the proletariat   The rule of the workers over the bourgeoisie.

Doctors' Plot   A group of prominent (mostly Jewish) Moscow doctors was accused of conspiracy to assassinate Soviet leaders, at the same time as anti-Semitic material was published in the media. Nine doctors were subsequently arrested, although after the death of Stalin the case was dropped due to lack of evidence and was later alleged to have been fabricated.

Dual Authority The sharing of power between the *Duma* and Petrograd Soviet which occurred after the abdication of Nicholas II in 1917.

Duma An elected imperial parliament with a restricted franchise.

Eastern Question The issues which arose due to the instability and subsequent collapse of the Ottoman state.

Egalitarian society A form of society in which everybody has equal rights.

Emancipation of the serfs The abolition of serfdom which was announced in 1861.

Five-Year Plans Economic plans which set targets for production based on a five-year cycle.

Fundamental Laws of 1832 Regulations that reinforced the autocratic position of the tsar.

Fundamental Laws of 1906 Regulations that reinforced the position of the tsar and specifically watered down the impact of the 1905 reforms.

Grain requisitioning The compulsory acquisition of grain by the state.

Great Russia The territory which formed the Old Russian Principality, focused on Moscow.

Great Spurt The increase in economic and industrial activity which occurred under Finance Minister Witte (1893–1903).

Great Terror The period from 1936 to 1938 in which the terrorising of the Russian people reached its greatest height.

Greens A general term given to peasant groups who opposed Bolshevik rule.

Gulags Labour camps which housed political dissidents and other people considered to be subversive.

Interior Ministry The Ministry of Internal Affairs (MVD), which dealt with internal state security.

July Days Demonstrations against the Provisional Government, followed by armed clashes between soldiers and industrial workers, in July 1917.

Kadets The Constitutional Democrats, a liberal political group which was founded in 1905.

KGB The Committee for State Security, formed out of the MVD in 1954. It focused on the internal and external security of the USSR.

Kornilov Affair An attempted coup d'état against Kerensky's Provisional Government by General Kornilov, Commander-in-Chief of the Russian army.

Kulaks A wealthy class of peasants.

Kuomintang A major nationalist party in China.

Land Captains Landowners appointed from 1889 onwards to oversee the work of *Zemstva*, the regional councils.

Liberal democracy A political ideology which promotes the right of people to be free to choose. It particularly promotes freedom of expression and the ability of the people to elect a government of their own choosing.

Manchuria A geographical region in north-east Asia.

Marshall Plan A programme to help European recovery after the Second World War which was put forward by the US Secretary of State, General George Marshall (1880–1959). He believed that the USA should 'assist in the return of normal economic health in the world, without which there can be no political stability and no assured peace'.

Marxism–Leninism Lenin's interpretation of Marxism.

Medele'ev tariff A 700-page book of tariffs which were to be applied to all imports of goods. It was introduced in 1891.

Mir Groups of elders who were responsible for monitoring the conduct of those who lived in rural communities.

MVD The Ministry of Internal Affairs, formed from the NKGB, the People's Commissariat for State Security, which was disbanded in 1946. Its role was similar to that of the defunct NKVD (1934–43).

National minorities Non-Russian ethnic groups which were spread across the Empire.

New Economic Policy (NEP) A policy which liberalised the economy. It was designed to counter some of the problems introduced by War Communism.

NKVD The People's Commissariat for Internal Affairs, formed by Stalin in 1934. It was essentially a secret police force.

October Manifesto   A blueprint issued by Nicholas II for a new form of elective government revolving around the *Duma*.

October Revolution   The 1917 revolution which brought the Bolsheviks to power.

Octobrists   Supporters of Tsar Nicholas II and particularly his proposals made in the October manifesto.

Ogburo   A body formed under the Central Committee which was responsible for maintaining order and dealing with opposition.

OGPU   The secret police formed from the Cheka and active between 1922 and 1934.

Okhrana   The secret police active under the tsarist regime.

Old guard   The incumbent political elite which represented traditional interests.

Orgburo   A body formed under the Central Committee which was responsible for organising party affairs.

Ottoman   A dynasty which had ruled an empire based around the modern state of Turkey (c1300–1922).

Pale of Settlement   A western region of Russia in which Jewish people were permitted to live permanently; beyond its borders they were generally excluded.

Party Central Committee   The main body responsible for the administration and operation of three political offices: the Politburo, the Orgburo and the Ogburo.

People's Will   A terrorist group formed in 1879 which aimed to initiate revolution through 'propaganda of the deed' (terrorism).

Permanent revolution   A political theory put forwards by Marx and Engels and then further developed by Trotsky. It dealt with the way in which a revolution could be achieved in countries which had not yet reached an advanced stage of capitalism.

Petrograd Soviet   The Petrograd workers' council, which was set up in early 1917 to campaign for workers' rights.

Politburo   A small elite group of Bolsheviks who were in charge of forming policies.

Populists   Russian intellectuals who attempted to challenge tsarist policy in the late nineteenth century. They aimed to educate peasants and promote a popular form of socialism.

Proletariat   The urban industrial workers.

Provisional Government   The temporary government which was set up following the abdication of Nicholas II in March 1917. It was overthrown in the October Revolution.

Purge   The removal of those considered to be political enemies through imprisonment, exile or execution.

Red Army   The communist army, mainly recruited from the soviets and factory committees.

Red Guard   A term which referred to armed supporters of the Bolsheviks, especially in the second half of 1917.

Red Terror   The fear which arose through the threat of arrest, imprisonment, exile and/or execution.

Redemption payments   The repayment of loans which had been used to purchase the land that had been redistributed after 1861.

Reform   To make a change to an existing set of policies and/or institutions.

Repression   The control, restraint, prevention or inhibition of the thoughts and actions of others.

Revolutionary defencism   The defence and protection of everything achieved by revolutionaries in February–March 1917.

Rus peoples   The Rus peoples were supposedly the original inhabitants of Russia.

Russian Orthodox Church   The official branch of Christianity in Russia. It was separate from the Roman Catholic Church and other branches of Christianity.

Russification   A policy designed to transform the different populations of the Russian Empire into 'pure' Rus.

Satellite state   A state which was heavily influenced by another state, in this instance Soviet Russia.

SDs   Those who belonged to the All-Russian Social Democratic Workers' Party, which was founded in Minsk, 1898.

Serf   A peasant tied to an agricultural estate owned by a noble.

Show trials   Trials of important political figures which were open to public view.

Single-party state   A single-party state exists where the government of a country is dominated by members of one political party and where there are no other parties to provide opposition.

Slav peoples   An ethnic group comprising peoples speaking a variant of the same Indo-European language.

Socialism in one country   A theory put forward by Stalin in 1924 that the USSR should focus internally because socialism had already been defeated in the other European countries.

Socialist realism The 'official' style of art and literature. It was designed to reflect the heroic efforts of workers and peasants.

Soviet A workers' council.

Sovnarkom The Soviet of People's Commissars, set up in 1917. This consisted of elected members who were given governmental responsibilities.

SRs Socialist revolutionaries who grew out of the Populist movement. They had a greater interest in the urban proletariat. The Socialist Revolutionary Party was formed in 1901.

Stakhanovite movement A movement based on the exploits of Alexei Stakhanov, a particularly industrious Donbas miner. He was promoted as a 'model' worker for others to copy.

Superstructure The ideology and culture which develop from an economic base.

Totalitarianism A form of government which includes total control of all aspects of the lives of the people by one authority (person and/or group). There is no toleration of dissent or opposition.

Treaty of Brest-Litovsk A treaty signed between Soviet Russia and Germany in 1918. Territory was given to Germany, and Russia also agreed to pay reparations.

Treaty of Friendship, Co-operation and Mutual Assistance (1948) The basis of post-war Finno-Soviet relations, 1948–92, under which the Soviets attempted to deter Allied attacks upon the USSR using Finnish territory.

Truman Doctrine In response to the prospect of communist governments being installed in Greece and Turkey, US President Truman declared in 1947 that the USA would support 'free peoples' who were 'resisting subjugation by armed minorities or by outside pressures.'

Universal franchise The right of all adult citizens to vote and elect political representatives.

Vera Zasulich case Vera Zasulich was a Russian Menshevik writer and revolutionary who shot and wounded General Trepov in 1878; she was later acquitted at trial.

Virgin Lands scheme Khrushchev's campaign to introduce agriculture to the 'virgin' soils of Kazakhstan and Western Siberia.

Wager on the strong A name for the Stolypin reform of 1906 which aimed to redistribute land to the more able and educated peasants.

War Communism The economic policies introduced during the Civil War. These included the nationalisation of large enterprises, a state monopoly of markets for goods and services, and the forced requisitioning of agricultural produce.

Whites A term which refers to those who opposed the Bolsheviks during the Civil War.

Zemstva Regional councils which were introduced by Alexander II in 1864. They were located only in areas considered to be part of Great Russia, and were dominated by wealthy landowners and the professional classes.

Key figures

Alexander II (1818–81) In 1855 Alexander II became tsar upon the death of his father Nicholas I. In 1856 the new tsar made peace with the enemies that Russia had faced during the Crimean War. In 1861 he introduced the Great Emancipation Statute. The Russian people seemed to welcome Alexander II as ruler and were generally happy with reforms that followed the emancipation of the serfs. However, the radicals were not impressed as Russia continued to be governed through autocracy. Ironically, just before his assassination in 1881 Alexander was about to sign an agreement that would probably have resulted in a more democratic government.

Alexander III (1845–94) Alexander III was a military man who believed strongly in autocracy.

His period of rule is often seen as one of reaction and repression in response to the more relaxed liberal period of governance under his father. He passed the Statute Concerning Measures for the Production of State Security and the Social Order and organised a Russification programme. He was intent on returning stability to Russia and on ensuring that social unrest and opposition to tsarism did not get out of hand. His reign proved relatively peaceful and some very positive economic reforms were carried out (especially the introduction of the Peasant Land Bank in 1883).

Leonid Nikolaievich Andreyev (1871–1919) A Russian playwright and novelist. He was the most influential member of the Expressionists, writers who focused on realism, naturalism and symbolism in their work. During the unrest of 1905 Andreyev campaigned for greater democracy and for improvements in the living and working conditions of the Russian people. However, he later became disillusioned with the Bolsheviks and became one of their most prominent critics.

Nikolai Bukharin (1888–1938)   Bukharin started his political career as a Bolshevik revolutionary before progressing to become a leading light in the Soviet government under Stalin. Bukharin helped Stalin to stave off opposition from Trotsky, Zinoviev and Kamenev, and was rewarded with the position of General Secretary of the executive committee of Comintern (1926–29). However, Bukharin opposed collectivisation and he fell out with Stalin. By 1937 he was so distrusted by the Russian leader that he was arrested, charged with conspiring to overthrow the Soviet government and executed in March 1938.

General Chiang Kai-shek (1887–1975)   A Chinese political and military leader, best known for his involvement with the Kuomintang (KMT), the Chinese Nationalist Party. In 1926 he became official leader of the KMT following the Canton Coup. He also worked as chairman of the National Military Council of the Nationalist Government of the Republic of China (ROC) from 1928 to 1948. He was generally a conservative, nationalist and believer in traditional values. He led in an authoritarian style and became an enemy of the Chinese communists, whom he viewed as a serious challenge to his position.

Friedrich Engels (1820–95)   Born in Barmen in 1820, his father was a wealthy German industrialist who owned factories producing cotton textiles in Manchester. In 1842, Engels was sent to Manchester by his father to gain an insight into the factory management. Appalled by the poor living and working conditions there, he wrote *The Condition of the Working Class in England*, an account of what he believed to be the failings of capitalism. He also wrote articles for the radical journal *Franco-German Annals*, edited by Karl Marx. When based in Brussels the two co-wrote a pamphlet that became *The Communist Manifesto* (published in 1848). The Manifesto set out some of the principles of communism and how the ideology was likely to lead to revolution. When Marx died in 1884 Engels spent much of his time, until his own death, editing and writing the last two volumes of *Capital*.

Wladyslaw Gomulka (1905–82)   A Polish communist who was instrumental in the formation of the Polish Workers' Party (1942). He became a key figure in the Provisional Government of National Unity (1943–48) but was denounced by opponents as a reactionary. In the early 1950s Gomulka spent time in prison; he was released as a result of de-Stalinisation and was elected as the leader of a new Polish government (1956–70).

Lazar Moiseyevich Kaganovich (1893–1991)   Kaganovich was a key administrator and associate of Joseph Stalin. He remained a Stalinist until his death in 1991.

Nikita Khrushchev (1894–1971)   From the death of Stalin, in 1953, to 1956, Khrushchev started to dominate the communist party and won the struggle for power against Malenkov and Beria. During the Twentieth Party Congress in 1956 he attacked Stalinism. This marked the start of de-Stalinisation. He promised a raft of economic and social reforms designed to raise living standards. Unfortunately, he struggled, against the backdrop of the financially crippling Cold War, to find the money to carry out his plans. He also suffered as a result of what some rivals saw as a liberal attitude and the image he portrayed as a man of the people. In the end it was relatively easy for his opponents to launch a campaign that secured his dismissal in 1964.

Vladimir Ilyich Ulyanov Lenin (1870–1924)   Lenin was born in Simbirsk (Urals); his father was a member of the lesser nobility and worked as a schools inspector. In 1887 the execution of his brother strengthened Lenin's will to change the way Russia was ruled. By the end of 1891 he had graduated with a law degree and had already become involved in radical politics. His political views led to his exile in 1897 – this started a pattern of exile and return that lasted until 1917.

Karl Heinrich Marx (1818–83)   Born in Trier in western Germany, the son of a successful Jewish lawyer, Marx studied law in Bonn and Berlin before entering journalism as a career. In 1843 he moved to Paris and engaged in radical politics. He became a revolutionary communist, collaborating with Friedrich Engels to develop communist ideology. Marx and Engels are probably best known for co-authoring the pamphlet *The Communist Manifesto* (1848), which argued that all human history had been based on class struggles which would eventually disappear once industrial proletariats had taken control of governments.

Anastas Ivanovich Mikoyan (1895–1978)   Mikoyan's career as a politician ebbed and flowed; he started as a staunch supporter of early Bolshevism before becoming a respected adviser to Stalin (at one point he was Minister of Foreign Trade). After the Second World War Mikoyan's relationship with Stalin soured; he was demoted but went on, after Stalin's death, to seek revenge of a kind by backing Khrushchev's de-Stalinisation policy.

Pavel Nikolayevich Milyukov (1859–1943) Milyukov is often discussed in the context of the growth of liberalism in Russia; he founded and managed the Constitutional Democratic Party (Kadets). However, during the rule of the Provisional Government, Milyukov made significant contributions to foreign policy, campaigning to ensure Russia's continuation of the First World War.

Vyacheslav Mikhailovich Molotov (1890–1986) Molotov held positions of significance in Stalin's Soviet government. He worked as Chairman of the Council of People's Commissars from 1930 to 1941 and, intermittently, as Minister of Foreign Affairs from 1939 to 1956. He is best known for his role as a diplomat in the signing of the Molotov–Ribbentrop pact of 1939 (also referred to as the Nazi–Soviet pact).

Nicholas I (1796–1855) Tsar of Russia from 1825 to 1855. His reign was marked by periods of social unrest (which was dealt with ruthlessly), a sluggish economy and an inefficient administrative system. Nicholas seemed preoccupied with attempting to maintain Russia's status as a major military power and with expanding its territory. However, the military exploits of the tsar came to a sticky end with Russia's poor performance during the Crimean War (1853–56).

Nicholas II (1868–1917) In 1894 Nicholas succeeded his father, Alexander III. In the same year he married the Princess Alexandra, the German granddaughter of Queen Victoria. In 1905 he famously announced the October Manifesto and a new constitution which resulted in the formation of the first *Duma* (1906). His mishandling of Russia's involvement in the First World War led to his downfall and the end of the Romanov dynasty.

George Plekhanov (1856–1918) A highly respected Populist and member of Black Repartition who was one of the first to be converted to Marxism (known as the 'father of Russian Marxism').

Konstantin Pobedonostsev (1827–1907) In 1841 Pobedonostsev enrolled at the St Petersburg School of Jurisprudence and by 1859 he had started teaching at Moscow State University, where he went on to gain a professorship. He helped in the preparation of Judicial Reforms in 1864, after which he went on to become tutor to Alexander II's sons (Nicholas and Alexander). In 1868 he was appointed as a Senator. He became a member of the Council of Empire in 1874 and his final significant position was his appointment as Chief Procurator of the Holy Synod in 1880.

Joseph Stalin (1879–1953) Stalin was born Iosif Vissarionovich Dzhugashvili in Georgia. In 1899 he was expelled from Tbilisi Seminary (a college for training priests) for his political views. By 1905 his political activities extended to representing local branches of the Bolshevik Party at conferences. Later, as leader of Russia, he was renowned for creating a totalitarian state through the ruthless use of repression.

Pyotr Struve (1870–1944) Struve started his political career as a Legal Marxist (that is, one who preached a form of Marxism that was acceptable in the eyes of the authorities). He later changed to become a Kadet and then a White during the Civil War.

Leon Trotsky (1879–1940) Trotsky was born Leon Bronstein, to a Jewish family in Ukraine. A very able scholar, he then quickly rose up the political ranks. Appointed chairman of the St Petersburg Soviet in 1905 as an SR, but like Lenin, faced exile (1907–17, to parts of Europe and the USA). Trotsky was best known for organising the seizure of power in 1917, as the chief Russian negotiator of the Treaty of Brest-Litovsk in 1918 and as the organiser of the Red Army. However, after Lenin's death, Trotsky fell out with Stalin and once again was exiled. In 1940 he was assassinated with an ice-pick in Mexico (under Stalin's instruction).

Kliment Yefremovich Voroshilov (1881–1969) Voroshilov was a military officer and politician who rose to positions of importance during the rule of Stalin. He is best known for gaining the highest military rank in the Soviet Union (a Marshal of the Soviet Union).

Timeline

1855	Accession of Alexander II – the 'Tsar Liberator'
1856	Defeat in the Crimean War
1861	Emancipation of the serfs
1864	*Zemstva* Law and legal reforms
1865	Censorship regulations eased
1866	First assassination attempt against Alexander II
1874–81	Growth of opposition groups: Narodniks, Land and Liberty, People's Will
1881	Constitutional proposals; assassination of Alexander II; the 'Reaction'
1883	Peasant Land Bank created
1887	Failed attempt to assassinate Alexander III
1889	Introduction of Land Captains
1891	Famine in 17 of Russia's 39 provinces
1893–1903	Witte's 'Great Spurt'
1894	Accession of Nicholas II
1898	Formation of Social Democrats (SDs)
1901	Formation of Socialist Revolutionaries (SRs)
1903	SDs split into Bolsheviks and Mensheviks
1904–05	Russo-Japanese War
1905	Bloody Sunday; 1905 Revolution; October Manifesto
1906–11	Stolypin's reforms
1906–14	Four *Dumas* met
1914–18	First World War
1917	February and October Revolutions

1917–22	The Civil War
1918	The Constituent Assembly; the Treaty of Brest-Litovsk
1918–21	War Communism
1921	The Kronstadt Rising; famine and economic collapse (up to c.6 million died of starvation and disease 1918–21)
1921–27	New Economic Policy (NEP)
1924	Lenin's death (struggle for power 1924–29)
1928–53	Stalin in power
1928–29	Introduction of the First Five-Year Plan and of collectivisation
1932–34	Famine (c.5 million died of starvation and disease)
1936–38	The Great Terror (reprised after the Second World War)
1941–45	The Great Patriotic War
1946	Censorship tightened; famine in Ukraine (1946–47)
1949	Leningrad purge; formation of Comecon
1953	Discovery of Doctors' Plot announced
1954–56	Khrushchev's rise to power (Stalin d. 1953); launch of Virgin lands scheme
1956	Denunciation of Stalin by Khrushchev (the 'Secret Speech')
1959	Khrushchev's maize-growing campaign launched
1962	Workers' riots in Novocherkassk; Cuban Missile Crisis
1963	Agricultural crisis generated by soil erosion on 'Virgin Lands'
1964	Fall of Khrushchev